Alan Bissett
Collected Plays 2009–2014

Alan Bissett
Collected Plays 2009–2014

**FREIGHT
BOOKS**

First published 2015

Freight Books
49-53 Virginia Street
Glasgow, G1 1TS
www.freightbooks.co.uk

A CIP catalogue reference for this book is available
from the British Library

ISBN: 978-1-908754-44-8

the publisher acknowledges investment from
Creative Scotland toward the publication of this book

Contents

All of these plays were directed by Sacha Kyle, except *The Ching Room* and *Jock*, which were directed by Cheryl Martin, *Jacquoranda*, which was directed by Kenny Miller, and *The Incredible Adam Spark*, which at the time of publication remains unproduced.

Introduction

I cannot lay any claim to have discovered Alan Bissett as a writer as he was already an established and popular novelist when I first approached him to write a play for *A Play A Pie and A Pint* at Oran Mor. But I admired his work and was able to offer him a platform to try his skills as a playwright. It was an opportunity he seized with enthusiasm. Indeed he took to theatre with relish and enjoyed the collaborative aspect of making a play happen hugely. His first play *The Ching Room* was a critical and popular success and went on to have many other lives beyond Oran Mor. It shares with all his work a zest for language, a sure feel for character and a strong moral purpose. It came as no surprise to me that Alan had admired the work of 7:84 and Wildcat and he is one of a number of younger Scottish playwrights in whose capable hands that tradition is thriving. Alan is the complete theatre man. I saw him perform *The Moira Monologues* at the Citizens Theatre and enjoyed his bold style so much that I cast and directed him in Gregory Burke's *Battery Farm* at Oran Mor. One of the great pleasures of producing plays at Oran Mor for me is a strong sense that a new wave of Scottish playwrights are taking our theatre forward in exciting new directions. Alan Bissett is at the leading edge of that wave.

David MacLennan
Producer *A Play A Pie and A Pint*

(9 June 1948 – 13 June 2014)

The Ching Room

By Alan Bissett

Sir?

    Oh! Sorry, I didn't think anyone was in here.

Quite alright, sir, in you come.

    Okay, thanks.

    Uh…

Sir?

    Well, I can't get in till you come out.

Aren't you coming in?

    Uh. Not while you're in it, no.

We seem to be at cross-purposes here, sir. What can I do for you exactly?

    Well, as I think I've made clear, I'd like to use this cubicle please. It's kind of an emergency.

I see, sir.

Uh. Were you about to go?

No, sir, no. I'm gone.

Okay then.

Well gone.

That's good. In which case.

Could you maybe…uh…leave me to it?

No can do, sir, no can do.

But this is the only cubicle, and I really need to go, and you're not *doing* anything so…

Not doing anything? On the contrary, sir. I am on official nightclub business in here.

I don't understand. Why would you need bouncers in the…toilet…cubicle?

Not a bouncer, sir, not a bouncer. Neither bruiser nor gorilla, I. My matters are more, shall we say, spiritual than that.

Well if you're not a bouncer....then what are you...doing here?

Oh come now, sir, I think we both know.

No. We really don't.

We're both aware what you're actually here for, sir.

I'm *actually* here to expel several pounds of fecal matter from my anus. I don't know what you're here for...

Are you serious, sir? You don't know where you are?

I thought I was in a nightclub toilet?

Oh no, sir, no. Perish the thought.

On Sauchiehall Street.

Not any more, sir, no.

Okay then. Where am I?

Come away in, sir, come away in. Helluva draught with this door open.

> Well, uh. I really should get back to my girlfriend. It's her birthday, you see, and…

I thought you said it was an emergency, sir?

> She's got a hat I could use…

You're quite safe, sir! This is a frequent problem I find in contemporary society, sir: *trust*.

Good.

> What are you locking the door for?

No reason to be afraid, sir, I merely stand between you and it so we will not be interrupted by scum and lowlifes. I feel certain sir shares my distaste for many of the fiends and vagabonds who walk the dancefloors of this establishment, not unlike creatures of the night in many respects. Don't you agree, sir?

> Of course. Uh. You always have to be careful of
>
> The wrong sort.

A crucifix and garlic one sometimes needs round here, sir! Now. Take a good look around. Is it coming to you?

No.

Oh baffled little sir. You make my heart gay with your naïvety! You, sir, have found your way to a place many think to be a mere myth. More mysterious than Atlantis, more wonderful than Narnia, more dangerous than the Bermuda Triangle. This, sir?

This. Is the Ching Room.

Ching room. What's a...what's a ching room?

Sir. Again you wound my sensitive feelings! Not 'a' Ching Room, sir, *the* Ching Room. Capital 'C', captial 'R'. Such are the ways in which it is differentiated from the many thousand inferior, knock-off ching rooms in nightclubs up and down this great nation of ours, run by toerags who believe in grubby material profit more than they do the quality of the great and holy Ching.

This, sir, is the room from which Ching first did emerge, spreading its own word, from heart to heart. The cradle, if you will, of civilisation.

O...kay. And who are you?

I, sir, am a mere servant of the Ching. Its priest, if you like. Its representative here on Earth.

I've...really...got to get back to my girlfriend. It's her birthday, you see, and she's already upset that I announced, quite loudly, to her friends that I needed a 'Number Two'.

Had quite a bit to drink you see. And this is all starting to make me a little bit...uh...

So if you don't mind....?

I'm sorry, sir, but once the threshold to the Ching Room has been crossed a transaction must take place, or else the cosmic balance of the Ching is disrupted. Do you want to be responsible for that, sir? Do you want to be responsible for tampering with the natural laws of the universe?

Uh, no, but I....

No.

I didn't think so, sir.

Now. You and I have what's known in the business as 'the business' to get down to.

Business?

Official Ching Business.

Look I really don't understand what's going on here and the thing is...the thing is...I've left my coat and the problem with some of my girlfriend's crowd is – well they're a rougher sort than you or I – and one of them's known to be a bit of a...'tea-leaf', you see. Different to my previous girlfriends, this one. Anyway my jacket is from Top Man, so it's quite expensive, and so I think you can appreciate why I *really* need to get back to it. Ha ha ha.

Ha ha ha!

Got ourselves in with a rough crowd, have we, sir?

      Well, they are an *earthier* lot than I'm perhaps used to, yes.

Wee bit out of our depth in a venue like this, are we, sir?

      Quite. One of those things.

Far cry from Hogwarts, is it not, sir? I did warn you about the type of lowlife *tramp* who frequents this establishment, did I not?

      Tramp? Now hang *on*. That's my *girlfriend* we're talking about.

Take it up the arse, does she, sir?

      Excuse me?

That crowd of hers out there. Mainly men, is it?

      Well, yes, as it happens.

Stop to wonder why that is, sir? Make you feel somewhat inadequate? You with your tiny, wee, middle-class goldfish member flopping away inside her gigantic ravine.

> Now listen here. I *really* don't think you should talk that way about wome-

No, *you* listen, sir!

Thank you.

Let me explain our so very cute little situation here, *sir*. There are certain – shall we say, metaphysical – issues you seem unwilling to face. You have reached the final stage in the evening's and – let's not understate here – *mankind's* evolution. You have ascended the levels, dodged the whirling chainsaws, leapt the chasms, and now, at last, you are ready to face the Big Boss.

> …big boss…?

Boss Ching.

> Boss Ching. Right. Could you just get out of the way of that door, so I could maybe…

When an architect, sir, first sat down to design this nightclub, him and his poofy interior designer pals sipping their lattes, could never have imagined that their vision would culminate in such an exclusive room as this. For only two people are allowed entry beyond the red ropes at any one time, sir, and those people are – at present – myself and yourself.

Boss Ching has arranged it thus.

Can I speak to Boss Ching?

Boss Ching will be here shortly, sir.

Can you tell me what he…looks like?

He is a white man, sir.

Can you maybe ask him to hurry up? I kind of need to go.

Hurry up? You don't hurry up Boss Ching, sir. Boss Ching hurries *you*.

But –

If you'll *just* let me get a word in, sir. There are soldiers – brothers to the likes of you and I, sir – on the frontlines of Iraq and Afghanistan who, as the Mujahidin rain holy Jihad upon their candy asses, talk through the tears about journeying home, tasting the sweetness of their girlfriend's mouth again, and one day, with the help from Lord God Almighty, the only being above Boss Ching himself, visiting this very room.

Even those presently feeding worms in the graveyard has heard of us, sir. You and I could go there this evening, sir, sprinkle Ching across the graves, and turn the place into the fucking Thriller video.

But first, sir.

First you and I have to do some business.

> Well, I definitely have to do some business, so if you don't
> mind…

Sir. If *you* don't mind. Would I come to your place of work, take down my pantaloons, and shite right there in front of you while you talk to a customer? While you sell him mobile *phones*? No, sir. I would not. You'd probably kill whichever impertinent cunt did that, would you not, sir? Who embarrassed you in your business-life to such a degree, would you not, sir?

> Well I-?

WOULD YOU NOT, SIR!

> Uh. I suppose I'm.
>
> Not needing
>
> To go.
>
> Anymore.

Such are the healing properties of Ching, sir.

Say, 'thank you, Ching Room.'

Thank you, Ching Room.

Ching Room says no problem at all, sir. Say 'Amen', sir.

Amen.

We are mere vessels for the Ching.

Uh, I'm sorry to insist upon this point, but can I just ask...

Sir?

What...is....?

What is Ching?

Exactly.

What is Ching, sir? What is Ching? This is the question which every man must ask himself on a Saturday night on the greatest boulevard the world has ever seen.

Sauchiehall Street?

Indeed, sir. Washed and blessed with Ching.

Yet what is Ching? What is the condition of Ching?

Ching is like coffee made from thunder, sir.

       Really?

It will make you shit rainbows.

Accept the love of the Ching Room and you will be rewarded with nirvana itself, sir.

Refuse the Ching Room and it will enact…

a terrible revenge.

       I see.

What's it to be, sir?

Pain or love. The Ching room dispenses both.

       Okay, back up there, bud.

Sir?

       Now just you wait. Just *hang on* a minute.

Hanging, sir, is not an advisable concept to suggest, in the-

-in the Ching Room. Yes okay, I get it.

You're a drug dealer, aren't you?

That is but one of the names which the Ching has chosen for me, sir.

But, like the Ching itself, I have many.

What's your real name?

Darren.

Darren. Hi. Rory.

Nice to meet you, Rory. I like your style.

Can't say the same. Now listen, Darren. Have I got this correct? I'm here to take what I can't refer to in any other way than 'a great big shit'. You think I'm here to *purchase* shit, but am too afraid to ask for it. That's the misapprehension we're labouring under here, am I right?

That seems to be the case, sir, yes.

I'm actually labouring under the weight of something quite different.

But. Are you telling me that should I elect to purchase some...

Ching.

Ching, yes, I believe you called it. Should I elect to purchase some 'Ching' I'd be assured of a happy time because the 'Ching' which you're selling is of a superior quality to that being sold in toilet cubicles elsewhere.

It's like the difference between Take That and Beethoven, sir.

Oh, quite the snob.
Am I also right in saying that should I decline the offer of the 'Ching' being so...cryptically...offered to me, that there may be some kind of...violence....visited upon me in the immediate future?

I think we might finally be reaching an understanding, sir, yes.

How much does it cost?

Well, sir, price is something which it seems almost sacrilegious to attach to a substance as pure and true as the Ching. It would be like wandering into the Sistine Chapel and asking the Pope how much did it cost to paint yer ceiling?

We're in a toilet.

On Sauchiehall Street.

I accept the basic reality of the situation, sir, yes.

How much does it cost?

Seventy pounds a gram.

What? That's outrageous!

Scuse me a second, sir.

Ih?

That you, Barry?

Fuck ye want?

Aye, well I'm daein business in here!

Whit?

Just fuckin stab them.

Naw naw, nae mair negotiations, Barry. Sickay hearin it.

I dunno, cunto, yaize yer fuckin loaf! Skin them alive if ye havetay, long as I'm paid, Barry.

Sorry for the interruption there, sir.

Some people, eh? Don't know the meaning of the phrase 'buying a dog but barking yourself.'

Where did we get to?

...mumble mumble....

Thirty pounds, thank you very much indeed, sir. The Ching Room welcomes you into its church. Now, if you'll just allow me to prepare the sacrament.

Was he, uh, was he a business associate of yours?

He'd like to think so, sir. But one prefers to think of him as something of an...employee. Ronald McDonald doesn't flip burgers himself, does he, sir? No, he has people to do that for him. Too busy with his children's parties.

Like this one.

Didn't he, ha ha...

Didn't he…

Read the job description?

They can be irritating when they simply fail to do the tasks for which they were hired. I mean, there was no mystery about it. Employee sought for up-and-coming new enterprise. Unsociable hours. Occasional knee-cappings. I mean, there are laws protecting workers from entering into contracts with employers where terms are unclear. So I think I've kept myself in the right, don't you, sir?

No troubles with the unions for you!

Quite.

Do you have difficulties with subordinates yourself, sir, in the, uh, bank…?

I don't work in a bank.

The estate agent's then?

You're way off.

Would sir care to make it apparent what the fuck he does for a living?

I'm a poet.

Ah.

Sir.

A poet.

Now it's all starting to make sense.

Make much money doing that, sir?

Out of poetry? You kidding?

Well we seem to be able to chuck seventy pounds about without too much care, don't we, sir?

And that – what's his face? – that Dr Seuss has done alright out of it, hasn't he?

I don't really publish that often. I'm, uh. I'm a wedding poet.

A wedding poet?

Bear with me here, sir, I'm not exactly up to date on current trends in the fields of literature. My hands are a wee bit dirtier than that, sir. Could you maybe explain to me what it is exactly a wedding poet does?

Okay, well you know how some people become professional musicians because they dream about being the next Jimi Hendrix or Kurt Cobain?

Here, sir.

The Ching.

'Smells Like Teen Spirit'.

HA HA HA HA!

ha ha

ha.

(cough) Well simply wanting to be the next big thing doesn't exactly pay the bills.

All have bills to be paid, sir. You're preaching to the converted.

So they join a band that does weddings. Y'know. Play 'Wonderful Tonight' and the Proclaimers and 'Congratulations', even if it's killing their soul, at least they're surviving on the thing they love the most. Y'know. Their music. Their art.

That's a rare thing, sir.

So...

I realised that there was a market our there for poetry at weddings. A lot of couples have a wee recital during their ceremony and I can write them a few lines. For a fee. For another fee I can even come to their wedding and read it aloud for them.

That right?

Get plenty work from that do we, sir?

Enough.

I like that, sir. Entrepreneurship. Engine of the economy, sir.. Little did I know you were one of my very own. Allow me to express my sincere admiration.

Thanks.

Would sir maybe…?

No.

What?

No, it's silly.

What is it? Go on.

Would you maybe recite me one of your wedding poems?

Recite you one?

Yes, sir. Just so one can understand the kind of thing sir means.

Well, I don't know. The circumstances are rather, unusual…

They are that, sir! On the other hand, the holy union of man and woman under God is not – if you care to stretch your imagination– so different to the transcendental union we will feel under the benevolent gaze of the Ching.

I'd be very grateful.

Okay. Um. Let me see if I can remember one…

HO!

FUCK OFF, CUNT, THIS CUBICLE'S BUSY!

AYE? WANTAY START LIKE! YE WANT A FUCKIN KNIFE THROUGH YER JAP'S EYE?

Shitein cunt.

Sorry, sir. Please. Continue.

Right. Uh. This one's called 'October Rain'.

It did not rain on the day I asked

If you would be my bride

And it did not rain on the day I asked

If you'd keep me warm inside

And it did not rain on the day I asked

If you'd wed my heart to yours

And it did not rain on the day I asked

If you'd keep us safe and pure

And if it rains, today, my love

As I take your hand in mine

I'll stand there soaking wet with you,

Until the end of time.

Hmm.

Sir.

That's really quite

Pish.

I know. I *know*. But that's the stuff they want.

With all due respect, sir? If you read that at my wedding? I'd jump up and down on your face.

> You'd have every right to. But believe me, when that was read at their wedding? You could have surfed on the floods of tears.

No accounting for taste is there, sir?

> Seriously, I've poured my heart out in these poems in the past, put everything into them, and they usually take one read of it and go, 'It's a wee bit…well…obscure.'
>
> So then I toss off something like 'October Rain' in four minutes and they go gaga.
>
> Philistines.

Still, though? You're contributing to somebody's big day, sir. That's a privilege. Know what I'm saying?

> Their big day. You should see some of their weddings! Chav-tastic. These big fat brides and their awful dresses and their pigshit-thick husbands and their bratty little white trash childr-

Oh, quite the snob.

See, sir, I'd like to think if I was in your position. Know, with a university degree and a gift with words, I wouldn't use them to patronise and condescend to ordinary people, people maybe not quite as fortunate as myself.

I didn't mean that. I meant-

Two people fall in love, get married, they want their day to be perfect. They're spending the rest of their lives together, they might want it to begin with a wee bit of poetry that sums up their feelings simply and clearly. Cos, y'know, sir, maybe the people at that wedding haven't got the time or the inclination or the education to sift through the many layers of meaning and symbolism and references to Percy Bysshe fuckin Shelley which you worked into your initial draft.

I appreciate that, I was just-

Maybe they just want to look at their Gary and their Lisa up there and hear some words that make them go 'Aww. Isn't that nice, Agnes? Til the end of time. And funnily enough, Agnes, it's raining the day. Dae ye see that? And that could've spoiled everything. But see that poem, he made it seem alright, know? Cos even if they're wet, they're wet the gither? Know, Agnes? Aw that was just right. Them words.'

Yes. I suppose you're right.

That said, let's not forget, sir, the standard of the poetry that you have visited upon the Ching Room here today. I mean, William McGonagall's got nothing on you, has he?

Yeah, okay okay.

The Ching Room hears all, sir.

It must remain untained by cunts prostituting their art just for the fuckin money.

Maybe no as different to that wee girlfriend of yours as you think, eh no sir?

Probably not, no.

Now.

Since we're finished our wee English lesson.

Maybe you might like to sample some true poetry.

Here.

Oh you want me to…?

Indeed I do, sir. Indeed I do.

Man writes poetry to become closer to God, does he not, sir? To become at one with his evironment?

…in some ways…

Well. Here are some lines.

…how do I…?

I'll show you. It's very easy.

Roll up a banknote like this, sir. Not that you've got many of them handy at the moment.

Press one nostril like this, okay? Bend your head down.

Put the banknote in your nose, put your nose to the line, and…

Ffffffffffff!

Ah!

that's the fuckin

Whoo!

Now, sir. Your turn.

Okay, I just…

That's it. Press your nostril.

and just…

Put your nose down, that's it, sir.

Yep.

I'll help you.

And now just.
           Fffffff!

That's it, sir.

That's the spirit!

        Oh.

        Oh lord.

Oh lord indeed, sir.

Can you feel the Ching possess you?

        This is.

        Um.

        Ooh!

You'll be speaking in tongues before you know it, sir.

Good stuff?

        It's not. Uh. It's not an unpleasant sensation, is it?

Gets better, sir.

Tingly.

Equips us with what we need to make our way in the world, sir. Allows us access to our truer selves. Unleashed. Uninhibited.

Yes, it's rather…?

It's *rather*.

Isn't it?

You feel it, sir?

Yes.

You feel that power coursing through you?

Oh. Quite.

That…poetry?

Poetry. Yes.

I'm a poet.

You are, sir.

You're the best fucking poet in the world.

I am!

Rabbie fucking Burns, sir? He was an amateur.

I am a good poet! I'm a great poet. Yeah. And none of them
know it!

Don't appreciate genius, sir

Yeah. I'm an artist. What am I doing pissing around with
fucking weddings? I should be *published*.

Have another line, sir.

Yeah.

Ffffff!

You like it?

Wonderful!

Let's hear it now, sir.

What?

Your poetry.

My poetry?

Raw.

Now?

Pure.

Again?

Uncut. Uncensored.

Improvised?

Straight off the top of your head, sir!

The real stuff?

Yeah! Feel it, sir. Deep in your soul!

Yeah.

Tear it out of yourself!

Yeah!

Fuck those bullshit weddings! Let me hear it. Let me hear it roar, sir!

Yeah!

Whoo!

My name is Rory. Now hear my story.

Yeah!

My surname's Harris. I've been to Paris.

(beatboxing)

When I rock the mike it feels like the shit.

Took it to my homies and it was legit.

dgt
I'm here with my woman she being a ho.

Ho!

Took it the Ching Room and Chinged with my bro!

Yo!
Rock!

(they both beatbox, then scat into…)

When you're on the Ching it's just the beginning and then pretty damn soon you're actually singing cos the Ching soul brother is bringing beginning and the sinning and winning is just what the Ching is.

Peace!

Yo yo yo.

Whoo!

My man!

Yeah!

You feel it?

Hell yeah!

Aye, it was still pish though.

You think?

Yeah. Total pish.

Oh. Okay. I was quite enjoying myself.

That's the main thing, sir. Ten out of ten for effort. We're getting there.

Yeah.

Good sounds, man.

Well. That'll be *my* arts education, sir.

Gotcha.

(Sniffs)

(*Sniffs*)

(*Sniffs*)

Any of that left?

In time, sir, in time.

(*Sniffs*)

While we're letting it all hang out, sir. How did you end up with this wee girlfriend of yours?

How does anybody end up with anybody? How did I end up here?

Pre-ordained, sir.

Ha ha. Quite.

But let's not avoid the question, eh? Forgive me for saying, but you don't seem very suited.

What makes you say that?

'I'm here with my woman, she being a ho!'

Ho!

Kind of a clue. Wee across-the-tracks thing you've got happening, sir?

You could say that.

And if I might be so bold, sir, I'm guessing she's a bit…younger than yourself?

What makes you say that?

Well. I don't really think a club like this is your, shall we say, natural habitat.

She's the babysitter.

Ah.

Sir.

Naughty boy.

My wife doesn't know.

Wouldn't imagine so, sir. Not the sort of thing one interrupts Coronation Street with an advert for, is it, sir?

Let me just throw this out there, sir. I'm guessing the wife's not a big fan of your poetry?

       …well she's stopped reading any of it, so…

She does have some taste then. None too fond of your cock either, sir, is she?

       Now look here!

Which makes the babysitter quite an attractive wee prospect, sir. That right? Flaunted herself a bit, didn't she? Tiny short skirts? Aye, I know the type, sir. We all know the type.

And I'm sure you don't make a habit of going out with her and her pals. That wouldn't be wise, would it? You mentioned something about a birthday. Have you and the wife have been dragged along? That's why you're in a place like this.

Is your wife out there, right now? At the same table as her? And the wee girlfriend's getting a bit pissed, isn't she, and she's not being very subtle about thi-

       No. My wife's not here. She was going to come, but I told
       her not to. Said it'd be full of kids. I'd turn up, show face,
       stay for a drink, then bugger off.

And yet here we are in the Ching Room, sir. At a quarter past one. Something's gone wrong with the plan. Something's forced you to stay.

Being a bit of a handful, is she, sir?

Yes, well. Things aren't really. Working out. Shall we say.

Feeling that one, sir, feeling that one. Speak to me, brother.

She. She has a.... roving eye.

Ah, they all do, sir, they all do. Remember what I said to you? About the basic problem of contemporary society?

What's that?

Trust.

This crowd of hers tonight. All these young boys. Thinking they're men. All over her. And she's loving it.

And there's nothing you can do about, is there, sir? Because you can't break cover. And there's too many of them anyway, and they're harder than you. And they're fitter than you, cos they're working boys using their hands and muscles. And they're younger and better looking than you. So you just have to sit there and take it, don't you, sir?

Fucking.

To *endure* it?

   Little

Am I right, sir?

   Bitch.

Now now, sir. Maybe you shouldn't talk that way about women

   She chased *me*. She chased me for *so long.*

That's what they do, sir.

   I told her no. Time and time again.
(*shakes head*)

   But every time she came back it'd be a lower cleavage, a flirtier wee glance. And then the texts started.

Texts, sir?

   Look.

Oh.

Oh that's.

That's very.

Inventive.

I can see why a poet could appreciate writing like that.

Wasn't making it easy for you, sir, was she?

Ach, there's only so long before you can go before you give in. I understand that, sir. Any man can understand that.

And now she's joking about telling my wife.

Joking, sir?

Except I know it's not a joke. She laughs about it, but I know what she's doing. She knows what she's doing. She uses it, every time she thinks I'm being too… possessive. Like tonight. If she thinks I'm getting out of line, she'll just…

Point to her phone.
That's what she does.

You really think she'd do it?

Hell yeah. Yeah I do. She's young. She doesn't give a fuck. She'd survive it, and I'd be blamed for the affair.

Sir's got himself into a bit of a mess, hasn't he? Sir's housekeeping hasn't really been upto scratch.

Tell me about it.

I'm with you, sir.

I am feeling it.

Let's take away this doubt and insecurity here, sir. Why don't you let the Ching work its divine magic one more time, eh? Go on. On the house.

Thanks.

The Ching recognises a brother in pain. You accepted him in, sir. You crossed the threshold and sealed the contract. The Ching Room protects its own.

Fffffffffff!

There you go, sir. That-a-boy.

Whoah.

This is.

Whoah.

It's fine, sir, just ride it. Just ride into it. Just let it take you. Let it be your friend.

Better?

Better. Cheers.

Let's lighten the mood now, eh? It's a Saturday, sir. The Ching Room's Holy Day. Its Sabbath. We shouldn't dwell on the negative, sir. Not on the Holy Day. Let's go back to the good place.

Yeah, please.

I want you to feel good about yourself, sir. The Ching Room wants you to feel good about yourself. The Ching Room wants you to come back. Again and again and again. This is why it provides the Ching. So what I want you to do, sir, is I want you to recite to me the poem – any poem – that you love most in the whole world. The one poem you wish you'd written. The poem that made you want to write poetry. That makes you...transcend...all these petty concerns.

You want me to recite it to you?

I do. I want to hear it, sir. I want to feel it.

Sure.

It's called 'Stopping By Woods on a Snowy Evening' and it's by Robert Frost.

You really want to hear it?

Absolutely, sir.

Well. I remember this from Primary School. Teacher read it to us. It was snowing outside. Few days before Christmas. Her voice. The whole lot of us still and listening.

Let me hear it, sir. Let it come.

> Whose woods these are I think I know.
> His house is in the village though.
> He will not see me stopping here
> To watch his woods fill up with snow.
>
> My little horse must think it queer
> To stop without a farmhouse near
> Between the woods and frozen lake
> The darkest evening of the year.
>
> He gives his harness bells a shake
> To ask if there is some mistake.
> The only other sound's the sweep
> Of easy wind and downy flake.
>
> The woods are lovely, dark and deep
> But I have promises to keep.
> And miles to go before I sleep.
>
> And miles to go before I sleep.

Sir.

That was.

That was the most beautiful thing I've ever heard, sir.

> You like it?

Like it, sir?

Words can't describe.

> Yeah. Well. I'll never get close to writing something as good as that.

But you *spoke* it, sir.

You spoke it and it went from you

Into me.

It passed between us.

That beauty.

Did you feel it?

> I felt it.

You were the vessel for it. *You*, sir. That makes you powerful.

> I suppose.

No, sir. No suppose about it. You moved me. You truly did.

It snowed on my wedding day, sir.

You were married?

Yes, sir. Hard to believe, isn't it? I remember waking up on the morning of it and…the whiteness…covering everything. All those filthy streets just made…white. The truth of that. It was like everything. Everything… bad…I'd ever done was being purified. By love. Like I was being

Forgiven.

And she was really beautiful too, y'know. On the day.

Aye. I was very happy that day, sir.

Very happy indeed.

I take it…it didn't…work out?

No, it didn't.

Right.

But it's fine. These wee problems go away. Eventually.

Aye.

Know something, sir. I'm really starting to quite like you.

Me too.

See when you walked in here, sir, I thought: what does this poof know?
No offence, sir.

None taken.

You just didn't look like you'd lived much, sir. That's all.

But actually see now, I'm thinking

You've lived just as much as me.

We're the same, you and me.

You feel it, sir?

I feel it.

That poem, man.
In fact, sir. In order to commemorate this moment. I'd like to give you
a wee gift.

No, no, it's fine, I really couldn't take any more Ching.

It's not the Ching, sir. It's not the Ching. It's a gift *from* the Ching. You
understand? You understand what I'm saying?

Not really, no.

See these people out there, sir. These others. You don't need them. The Ching Room speaks, and I hear what it says. Its representative on earth, see?

I'm not following.

There'll be no repercussions.

Repercussions to what?

The Ching Room, sir. The Ching Room can make this wee mistake of yours go away.

No, no don't do that, don't-

No no, it wouldn't do *that*. I thought we'd established at the start – I'm a sensitive soul. I sat there and appreciated your poetry, did I not? I felt it move me. Deep inside.

This is what the Ching can do for you, sir.

It removes *doubt*.

It removes *all traces*.

What are you proposing?

Oh, it's not me, sir.

It's the Ching Room. It makes the decisions here. But it does not like to be refused. It does not like to be rejected. These are not fitting responses to its love.

What would you do?

Just send a wee message. That's all. Almost like a wee hello from the Ching Room.

There's a certain arrogance creeping into her behaviour, I'm sure you'll agree, sir. People say that the Ching encourages arrogance, but it does not. It corrects arrogance where it finds it. The same way we have been humbled together here this evening.

You felt it too, sir. You told me you did.

No traces?

Like snow.

And maybe if the Ching Room makes this wee problem go away, you might have to do something for it one day. Just a wee thing. Nothing that'll trouble you too greatly. Something…ceremonial.

Not much to ask for having your eyes opened, is it?

But you're not going to-

Not if you don't want us to, sir. You're in charge here.

Just a wee message.

In whichever form the Ching Room feels it appropriate to take, sir.

And all your troubles will just disappear.

Divine intervention.

Something like that, yes.

Don't forget your gram, sir. You've paid for it.

Thanks.

Now go back. Go back out there. And while you're sitting there listening to it all, watching them mock you and ignore you and disrespect you, you'll know. Deep inside.

You'll feel that poetry.

That *power*.

Yes.

Yes.

Listen, man. Thanks for all of this. It's been good to talk to someone about it. Maybe I'll see you again sometime.

Oh I have no doubt, sir. Be waiting for me.

Goodbye, sir.

Bye.

Say, 'Thank you, Ching Room.'

'Thank you, Ching Room.'

Say, 'Amen,' sir.

Amen.

I remain your humble servant.

Sir.

END

TURBO FOLK

by Alan Bissett

CAMERON   **MIKO**   **VLAD**

Wow, this place is great. Lo fi!

So this is where the locals hang out?
No tourists?

                    No tourists will come here.

Not surprised.

That street looked kinda shady.

"Say hey babe.
Take a walk on the wild side…"

                    People have to make living.

What's this part of the city called anyway?

                    It doesn't matter.

                    You said come somewhere
                    you would not be recognised.

Aye it was a bit mad outside that hotel, eh.
I mean, have those girls not got homework to do?

Which girls?

Those wee fans that were standing outside.

Trying it on as we were getting into the car?

They were not fans.

'Oh baby, we lovaz you.
We showz you za real good time, honey to za bee.'

Ach, they'll get over me.

But this…aye… This feels a bit more real.

Glad you like it, sir.

Hey, Miko, I've told you,
there's no need to call me sir.

Where I come from people don't
stand on ceremony with each other.

Ah, then Scottish is good peoples, yes?

Yeah, we're a very…tolerant race.

And when you think about it really,
we both work for the same company.

Just that one of us is in marketing
and the other is…the marketed.

           I suppose that is true

So here we are…
in the market-place.

           We would not be able to sell you here.

No?

           Not while you are dressed like that.

           Would you like drink?

Aye, cheers. Whisky please.

           <Tva whiska, pallo.>

                <Zaaar. Nae probz.>

           Flavour?

What have they got?

Talisker. Macallan. Highland Park.

Not a bad range.

Whisky popular here.

No wonder, when it's so cold!

Make it a Jura. Single malt.

<Zyik that yin, pallo.
Jura. Twa. Aye.>

<Zerya go. Neebor.>

<Sanka.>

Just like being in the Clansman.

Clansman… is bar of Scotland?

Yeah. Dundee. My home-town.

Good whisky, good company,
and if there's a ceilidh band playing
you get an awfully good racket too.

Cay…lee?

Traditional Scottish music.

Drums, accordian.
Deedle eedle eedle.

Ah. The music of the people.

Aye, folk music.

It is harmless?

Well, I suppose you could be elbowed in the
face by a fiddler, but that's about it.

This music it is not

dangerous?

Think there's a wee problem with your English here, pal.

'Harmless' 'Dangerous.' It's just music. See what I mean?

Ah, but not all music
is just music.

Not according to the NME.

Enemy?

NME.

Enemy? Like gun? Bang bang?

For godsakes.

No, the N.M.E.

It's a *magazine*.

Magazine? Ah of course,

famous British NME.

No more rock dinosaur!

New look! New sound!

Exactly.

Sorry, I mistake. Here in this country
we have had real enemy.

You've never been reviewed by them.

No, was guns. Bombs.

Aye, sorry, I shouldn't joke.
I know you've had troubles here.

Yes, review. Let me do remember.

"Scottish   singer-songwriter,   Cameron
Campbell, reneges on his early promise with an
album aimed squarely – and I stress "squarely"
– at people who buy their music in ASDA.
While Campbell may be happy to hear one
of these songs being butchered eventually on
X-Factor, we can only hope that he rediscovers
the spark that made his early singles so exciting.
In the meantime, at least you know what to get
your dad for Christmas."

The NME. No?

Well remembered.

Is job.

Perfect English.

Is no guns and bombs.

No, suppose not.
Should look on the bright side eh.

Yes. You are man who get up in morning, and
play music.

But I mean, it sold! That's the main thing,
the bloody thing sold!

Our mutual employer was happy.

Very happy.
I read emails from UK office.

Throw the party!
Cameron Campbell!

Number ten in charts!

Listen, that's not bad in an age when apparently
nobody wants to pay for music anymore.

Somebody needs to tell these critics:

You don't get to play the main stage at T in the Park
unless there's a lot of paying punters out there who love you.

And I mean *love*.

        Drink to that.

Nice one. Slainte.

        Huh?

It's traditional. In Scotland.

        Ah okay. Slainte.

        Mm.

Good, isn't it?

        Is beautiful.

Hey, check out that barman's shirt.

That is one really cool shirt.

Is also beautiful.
But I prefer whisky.

Actually, I need to pick up something to wear
onstage tomorrow night…

Where do you think he might have bought that?

I have no idea.

Hey, mate.

<Za?>

I like your shirt.

<Vit?>

Your shirt. I really like your shirt.

<Diznat spack Anglish, pallo.>

This. I like it. Thumbs up!

< Diznat teesh ma shyeert, cantyboz.>

Beautiful.

<Vit?>

Em. WHERE DID YOU BUY IT?

I think now you should leave him alone.

<Poofta.>

What's his problem.

He cannot understand you.

I just wanted to tell him he had a nice shirt.

Best to leave. Come.

Obviously not used to tourists.

<Or bawbagz…>

What?

No. No tourist here.

<Hey! Chyiz!>

Em. Cheers!

Band playing music soon.
You will like.
This way. Stage.

A band, aye?

Rock n roll? Jazz? Blues?

> Ah, is like music you say in bar in Scotland.

Traditional?

> Yes. Of the people.

> Is folk. But volume? Turbo folk.

Turbo folk?

> Like Bob Dylan. The electric.

> "Judas!"

Oh right, I see.

'Turbo folk.' I like the sound of that.

Well., Miko, that's why I wanted to come out tonight, know?

New music, new experiences, all good for...
filling up the well

> Well is dry?

Not for long.

gmp
Another drink?

> Uh yes...(sigh)

<Nyer twa whiska, pallo.>

> <Nyer twa? Hmph.
> *Zee* gontay buya glugo?>

<Zyek. Talma bootet.>

Know what, it's good to actually get out
and *see* this place.

Hotel. TV studio. Gig. Airport.
Gig. Radio interview. Gig.

'Mr Campbell, what do you think represents the sound of Scotland?'
'Police sirens. Next question.'

So I'm sitting there in yet another hotel bar
watching yet another match involving two European teams
I know absolutely nothing about except
their names don't rhyme with *anything*.

and I thought
know what?

See for just one night?

I want to get a bit…
closer to things.

Smell the *truth* of a country, know?

> You will smell that here.

Em. What country are we actually in again?

> You are very funny for Britishman.

Scotsman.

> To me is same.

Anyway thanks for coming out with me.

> Is job.

Aye, but there's probably things you'd
like to be doing tonight, and you're
having to hang out with a client.

I mean, are you not married?

> My wife…she used to it.

> Before, I was in army. So this
> more preference to her.

You were in the army?
What was that like?

> Let us say is better working for record company
> than fighting war.

I can imagine.

No. You cannot.

Well, Miko?
Here's to survival

What did you survive?

The tour.

(sigh)

Okay. Slainte?

Slainge indeed!
Aah!

gnmp

Burns, doesn't it?

Like Rabbie!

Ha ha, good one.

Ah, the band is making entrance now.
This man, very good guitar.
You watch.

Yeah! Turbo folk!

Whoo!

The sound of the people, eh Miko?

Cannay beat it, whatever country you're in.

                                                                <Ak. Bletherecn gay.
                                                                  Zut! Zut!>

                        Shit.

What's that?

                            <Soko nervista. Dane ma heid in, pallo.>

I don't. Speak. Your language.

What's he saying?

                            He's just wondering if you
                            can keep it down so he can
                            hear the band?

Oh aye, sure, no problem.

                            <Excusisto. Touristaz, ken?
                            Numpty.
                            Dane ma heid in tay!>
                                                        <Britiz?>

                          <Scottiz.>

                                        <Iz zame heeng, naw?>
                      <Zyet.>

                                  <Breetez. Poofay poofay.
                                    Teesh ma shyeert?

Naw!
Nae way.>

<Oka.>

What's he saying?

We are just conversing about this band.
He doesn't like their new album.

He seems pretty angry about it.

He is a big fan.

I remember when I used to feel like that about music.

Saw U2 at Celtic Park. 1993.
I was only 15.

All those thousands of people. And one man,
just one man controlling
what they thought
what they felt.

Yes, we have had that in this
country too.

U2 played here?

No.

Anyway,

I saw him standing there, this tiny figure on a stage.
Everyone just…giving themselves to him.

And I thought: the power of that.

Bono save world.

Perhaps now we should concentrate
on the-

You'll never feel as passionately about music as you do
when you're fifteen.

When I was fifteen.

Hm.

<Litt! You tva bawbags.
Yappa yappa.
Kveed!>

<Excusa.>

Good band eh!

<Vit?>

Turbo folk! Big thumbs up!

<Vit yappa?>
Cool shirt!

<Zay teesh ma shyeert.
Hofannay.>

<Tourista ken? Excuse, neebor.>

<Bvat bvat smacko doof!>

<I zpika tay him.>

<Yat! Lasto varneen.>

Wow, he's really passionate about that band.

Listen,
you should stop the touching of his shirt.

But did you tell him I like the shirt?

That's what I'm trying to communicate to him.

He is not interested. He just warn
you to stop touching it.

He warned me?

Oh no no, he's got it all wrong.

        No, I would leave. Serious.

Listen, pal.

                <Zar?>

I didn't mean anything by it.

Only touched your shirt as a compliment.

No hassle here.

                <Votto?>

        <Shyeert coolio...>

                <Zay poofta?>

        <Um. Mebbes. Em...
Lika Ziggy Stardoost?>

                <Hyem?>

        <Bi?>

                <Aska aska!>

What's he saying?

        He says he want to know if you have
sex with another man in the ass?

Um.

I mean, I don't know him very well,
so uh…

He is not making proposition.

You understand?

He is angry like the wasp.

Oh, I see.

Then I think it's best if you tell him no.

<Naw poofta.>

<Goot!>

<Tello him glug glug
maka mya steeeemboats.>

He wants you to buy him drink.
Uh. Sure.

What would he like?

<Scottiz vhiska!>

He wants you to make selection of
The Scottish whisky that is the most mwah!
Special.

Most special! No problem.

<Ziska buddy? Neebor? Pallo?>

<Gotta loombared. Geez a break!>

<Ha ha>

<"Go to the place where you
make the toilet with your anus.">

<Lika Borat?>

<Ha ha ha.>

<Ha ha ha ha ha.>

Uh, sorry to interrupt.
Will this also be covered by the record company?

None of this is paid for by record company.

So who pays for it?
                    I do.

Ah, Miko…I'd help you out,
but I don't have any currency.

Usually the marketing guys always…
Y'know.

<Zar….eejit….>

So I suppose I must pay for this also?

If you could. Um.
Just get him one of the cheap ones.

He won't know.

<Vhiska. Grantz.>

Fine country you have here!

<Vatta yaboo the noo?>

<Gon mental zi coontra.>

<Ha! Zo. Gon mental zi coontra?
Hyam Britiz.
Simbat wiv zat,
Solla vocho cho cho

heed the baw?

Gava boom
bang

Deedo.>

He says thank you.

Ah, no problem.

Anytime! Cheers!

<Huh. Chyiz.
Britiz. Scottiz.
Zey keel.
Zey keel.
Myoooordoraaaaaaz.>

He's really fired up.
What was all that about?

Oh, is nothing.

He is merely pointing out that you

British only stopped occupying us

thirteen years ago.

Really?

Yes. During the 'peacekeeping'
<Familia? Vorjack?>

<Zyet.>

in which some of his family were killed.

That sort of thing.

Oh.

Um.

Do not worry.
Long time ago.

Not for me.

Do you…
Do you speak English?

No.

heh heh

Ah! This good song.

What's it called?

Is called

'She Leave Me So I Shoot Her'

That right?

Is very passionate love song.

Very passionate.

<Shya lyav meeee

Zo I shyeot hoir!>

<Zat crazy beetcho.>

<Takka zee kyeedz>
<Takka zee doyg>

<Woof woof!>

<Shya lyav meeeee>

<Zo I shyeot haar!>

Um.

<Zyen?>

<Nineteen Ninety Three!>

Guys?

<Shya lyav meeeee>

<Zo I shyeot hoir!>

I'm just going to the toilet.

Sure.

You couldn't...
get me another drink?

<RAT A-TAT A-TAT>

<AT-AT AT-AT AT-AT AT-AT>

Actually I'm fine.

(exits)

*I miss that soft, sweet
woman…*

*Soooooooooo
much.*

Ha ha ha ha ha.

Heh heh.

It's a good song.

From the heart.

Listen, my friend.

My companion, the Scotsman,
He doesn't know what he's doing,
But he means no harm.

So what *is* he doing
in here?

Doesn't he know what kind of place this is?

He sees only our

native hospitality.

Ha. Are we *in* a hospital?

No.

So I ask again: what's he doing here?

He's on tour.

Tour?

No, not *that* kind.

He is a famous singer
over in Scotland.

But he's not in Scotland though.
Is he?

Which is the problem with
the last lot of them who were here.

They were in *our* country.

That has nothing to do with him.

What are you even doing with this clown?

Officially? I am helping him
'discover our culture'.

Unofficially?

It looks like I am helping
him to get drunk.

Is that so?

Well.

I am all for strengthening relations with
our European brothers.

Please.

This is my livelihood.

You know how things were after the war,
it took me a long time to *get* a job like this.

We are not looking for trouble.

I'm sure those British soldiers
who took over this very bar
with their drunken songs
and their beatings for anyone
who dared to ask them why
they were here.

Were not looking for trouble either.

But they found it.

This is all in the past.

It is people like you who
will not let our country
move forwards.

Become whole again.

Know something, friend?

I'm sure I recognise you from somewhere.

Where did you grow up?

Graatz

Near the Zhetyn farm?

Yes.

I remember.
They called you the Little Cobra.

You're thinking of someone else.

Because of your *eyes*.

click click

No.

Look at me.

Leave me alone.

Look at me!

Fuck you.

Ah.
It *is* you.

Listen, *comrade*.

Now I work for a record company.
Good job. Nice wife. Own home.

That might sound *gay* to you and your...
brothers, but I went through
the same shit as the rest of you did.

I had enough.
I'm asking you, please let's not go back there.

Mph.

Now you are bringing
this *singer*. Their...culture.

It's just music.

to our homeland?

Heh heh.

My friend.

You can wear their t-shirt.

But you'll always be one of *us*.

Hey.

<Ziko.
Vilcom, howya dane?>

Heys. My main man!

<Letta zuska dronko glug glug?
Gatta pished!>

(shrug)

He wants to buy you drink.
To thank you for your earlier...

generosity.

<Scottiz!>

One from your homeland.

Aw, thanks mate.

<Zutto problama.
Fire in neebor.>

See? I'd heard that about this country:
that your hospitality was very Scottish.

heh

We are friendly nation too!

<Zyit?>

<Janta. Scottiz pallo pallo veka
'all nations'.>

<Pallo?>

Ha ha ha ha ha ha HA HA HA
Ha HA HA HA HA

hee

hee

Everything okay?

hee

hee

Yes, he like your Scottish humour.

Ah, I see. We're well known for that.

Our gallusness.

That's why every country loves us
and hates the English!

That and our music, of course,
even if I do say so myself.

>   <Ah. Zyee moozik.
>   Scottiska?
>   Yordaz playa?>

He wants to know if you play.

Oh.

Well, heh. I do have a certain
reputation
in my home country, yes.

>   <Yook.
>   Playay ze Turbo Folk
>   vitta zoska.>

        <Zerioosko?>

>   <Brodo latta zokonto band.
>   Vill sort it oot.>

Where's he going?

>   His brother, he is in the band.
>   He wants you to sing them a song.

He wants me to..?

No, I'm here incognito tonight.
I want to get away from all of that.

>   <Zisk! Zisk!
>   Famoosa Scottiz sangar.>

You are being introduced from the stage.

Am I?

<Guitara.
To hyim.>
Ja.>

They all want you.

Oh, *do* you now?

You want a quick…?

Oh well.
Maybe just one, eh.

…ooh nice guitar.
is it in tune…?
yeah?

<Scottizka Turbo Volk!>

Can you play some
Scottish music?

Right.
This is from my recent album *Peach Melba*.
It's about a guy who loves a girl
But she doesn't love him back.

It's called 'Nothing Hurts…Except the Pain'

<Akak! Baws! Scottizka Turbo!>

No, they do not want to hear one
of *your* songs.

They want to hear 'traditional'.
The real music.

Let us know the Scottish peoples.

<zyaaaaar>

Ah, gotcha.
Let me think…

Okay. This one's called 'Bonnie Dundee'.

It's a regimental march.

<Arma chanto.
Trat trat trat trat.>

<Scottiz arma?

Ek!

Tikeen pish?>

How does it go…? Em.

Tae the Lords o convention twas Claverhouse spoke
E'er the King's Crown go down there are crowns to be broke
So each cavalier who loves honour and me
Let him follow the bonnets o Bonnie Dundee.

Come fill up my cup, come fill up my can
Come saddle my horses and call out my men
Unhook the West Port and let us gae free
For it's up with the bonnets o' Bonnie Dundee

<Scuza. Hey.
Niy niy niy.>

What's the matter?

                                        <Arma chanto?>

This is song of army?

Aye. Scots Guards.

                                <Aska. Skottizk Arma? Tsh!>

Were you in Scottish military?

No, but my Uncle Tam was. He used to sing this
to me and my brothers.

Made us march up and down the room,
saluting him.

I was high on Ribena. Loved it.

                                <Familia chanto.
                                Arma chanto.
                                Seenga laka
                                pwoofh! pwoofh!

                                teet teet teet
                                eee eee eee>

Ha ha ha.

What's so funny?

He says you sing like small girl.

Excuse me?

       Song for army marching?

       About family? Blood?

       Fighting enemy of homeland?

       You sing like small girl

                                                 <weeva>

       with

                                            <Swish! Swish!>

       pigtails.

Is that right?

                                            <teet teet teet
                                               eee eee>

Aye, well. Listen.
The pair ay yese.

My uncle served in the Argylls
for twenty five year. Proudly.

Fought in Argentina and Belfast.

                                          <Zo?>

Zo! Listen to his song, right?

                                      <Maka mya belyev.>

Make him believe.

Aye, I understood that just fine, Miko.

Yese think I'm no uptay it?

Any of the rest of you think I'm no uptay it?

Want me to keep gon? Aye. Good.

Dundee he is mounted and rides up the street
The bells tae ring backwards, the drums tae are beat
But the provost douce man he says, 'Just let it be.'
When the toon is well rid o' that devil Dundee.
Come fill up my cup, come fill up my can
Come saddle my horses and call out my men
Unhook the West Port and let us gae free
For it's up with the bonnets o' Bonnie Dundee

<Et. Et.>

<Pf.>

Whit is it noo?

<Saya maka mya belyev.>

You said you would make him bel-

Believe. Aye.

I heard him.

Listen, mate.

You know I've played the Main Stage
at T in the Park?

               (shrug)   (shrug)

The. Main. Stage.

               (shrug)   (shrug)

Aye awright,
it was at half two in the afternoon.

But still! Ken?

fuckin

There are hills beyond Pentland and lands beyond Forth
Be there lords in the south, there are chiefs in the north
There are brave downie wassles three thousand times three
Cry hey for the bonnets o' Bonnie Dundee

               \<Bettoro...\>

                            \<Brava brava!\>

Come fill up my cup, come fill up my can
Come saddle my horses and call out my men
Unhook the West Port and let us gae free
For it's up with the bonnets o'

                            \<Bonniez Dunday!\>

Then awa tae the hill to the lee and the rocks
Ere I own a usurper I'll crouch with the fox
So tremble false wigs in the midst of yer glee
For you've no seen the last of my bonnets and me

Come fill up my cup.

> <Come feyl up my kyan!>

Come saddle my horses.

> <Aynd kaal out my myen!>

Unhook the West Port.

> <Eh let uz giz freeeeeeee>

For it's up with the bonnets o Bonnie Dundee

> <Ya dansa!
>
> Brav brav!>

He is very impressed.
I am too.

Aye. Just as well.

> <Ye myka mya belyev.>

I made him believe?

Yes.

If only the NME could see
you now eh?

Too right. Aye.
Stick *that* up yer Asda.

<Skotsa. Eh? Brav.>

Scotland the Brave.

Aye, ye're welcome.

Ye want me tay sing somethin else?

No.   No.

Right. Well. Thanks for the lennay the guitar.

Quite enjoyed that. Whoof! No felt like that for a while.
Thanks everybody!

You're very special.

Especially *you*, madam...

Ah.
I so glad we is all now friends.

<Comrado?>

<....comrado...>

yes uh

I believe it is...my round.

As you say in Britain!

Scotland.

Yes, Scotland.

<Skotska. Goot.>

Scotland. Good. Aye.

I'm glad you agree.

A proud people, ken?

Don't like to see our heritage *mocked*.

heh heh

Ken whit, Miko?
I'll have a double whisky.

A…double.

<Dooblo?>

<Tva TVA vhiksa…>

<Ah. Nae probz.>

Skotska muzyak.
Mwah! Mwah!
Brava.>

You like that, aye?

<Aaaaaaay...>

Aaaaaaaay....

Ha ha ha.

Heh heh heh.

<Arma?>

Eh?

<Arma? Bang bang?>

Oh right.

No, I wis never in the army.
UNCLE.
Scots. Guards.

Never mind.

WERE YOU EVER IN THE ARMY?

<Eh? Ma arma?>

Aye. Were you...bang bang?

Ah. Yisk.

Nineteen nineties.>

Nineteen nineties.

Ah. That's when the British were occupying this place?

Still though.

I heard youse were uptay aw sortsay dodgy
shit round here, eh?

Heh heh heh.

<Vit?>

What did you say?

I'm just saying likes.

Heh heh.

If yese werenay uptay anythin
we wouldnay have been here, would we?

<Vit?>

Naughty naughty!

Heh heh heh

heh

he

<gvvvvvv...>

And what do you know of this?

Ho. Hang on, I'm just kiddin yese on.

What age were you?

Back then? Dunno.
Fifteen or sixteen.

<Sezis vanka!>

Do you know what I was doing

when I was fifteen?

Naw, eh…

I was in militia unit, protecting
hills around my father's farm.

From enemy who wanted to kill us.
I was night patrol.

Because my eyesight.

On the farm we have many rats.

And because I has such *skill* at spotting rats.

They called me the Little Cobra.

I

see

you

Yaaaagh!

!!!

When *you* were fifteen-

<Bono. Savez. Varld.>

You were in love with
pop stars.

Heh heh heh.

Aye.

Well. Listen.

Bono's a man who made stadium
rock into a new artform.

He's no a *pop star*.

<Zay?>

<Ha ha. Zyez. Bono zeela
rocka stadyoom Picasso.->

<Oh! Mezybez Michael Jackson
eza la Malcolm X?>

Aye, and I'm sure in this country
youse aw understaun aboot music.

Hammerin fuckin sheet metal aw day.

Ya coupla bastards.

Whaur's that double whisky?

Here.

Cheers!

Slainte.

fuckin
Had a gid wee laugh at ma expense,
have yese, Miko?

No, sir, ha ha.
It is not like that.

gnmp

Yes.

Aye, well. Know whit?

Please. Is fine. We all just make joke.

This is a fuckin shite country.

Heh heh heh.

Yer food's rotten.

Sir. Please, calm down.

Yer women are mingin.

That is enough now, please-

And I know fine well what happened here,
ya bunch of murderin bast-

HO.

ek!

miko

gonnay

kf

ek

let me go

cannay

breathe

Of course.

thanks

heh

gasp

wheeze…

cough!

(beep)

<Hallo? Ja. Isis here.
Za Breeteesh manna yappa yap
veziz myordoraz.
Scoom.

Oza…
Em. Lama theenko>

…fuckin maniacs…

<Oka.

Tekit ootside.
Ovnat.

Click click.

Deedo.>

(beep)

<Yisk?>

<Ja.>

Excuse me.

I am going outside.

I need breath of fresh air.

(exits)

Cough

<Vhiksa.>

Whisky?

<Ja.>

No problem.
Enjoy.

<Throatska gek gek.
Miko zuppa tay hi doh.

Kalaka.
Meh canno breffo!

Youzay gon geez gid dooan?

Meh tourista ken.

No kenna bettaro neebor.>

                       So we are murderers.

<Myord...?>

                       Murderers aye.

<Myordoraaz?
Niy niy. Listo.
Le Breetesh govamun
Zay yappa yappa.

Tokka zay

"Oh izza commyoonisto.
Comrade comrade. Bang bang.
Evel.">

                       Evil?
                    We are...evil?

<*Za* zaya evel. Govamun!
Ve gontay do eh?

Zay yappa.

Propa za ganda.

Ve belevska.>

                       Belevska?

<Ja. Belevska?>

Believe…?

Ah, I see you *believed*…your government.

<Za?>

Heh heh.

The sweet little fairy stories you British people
are told.
by your leaders.

Of innocent Red Riding Hood.

and the Big Bad Wolf.

<Volf?>

Wolf. Aaargh.

<ek>

This country is not innocent, no.

You have seen that already.

No-one who fought in that war
Can remain truly innocent.

But your country.

Your country fought in that war too.

So you cannot be Little Red Riding Hood
either.

Do you believe *that*?

<Belevska!

Lookeh.
Zi joosta playa moozik>.

Music?

<Moozikso.>

Ah, but this music you play.

This music is not innocent.

<Mookzika moozika!
Peach Melba noomero tyen.

Justa vonto bya lakka lakka

Yoo! Too!

Lakka ze Celtic Parka!>

Sorry, what?
Sel. Teec. Parka.

<Eh. Bigga geegzo.
Rocka rolla geegzo.
Za stadyoom!

Cameron Campbell!
Gonza big man!
Gon yersel. Ho!>

What are you talking about?

<Plez. Jusa mooziko.>

Music. Yes, what about it?

<Belyev.>

Believe?

<Ja! Mooziko belyev.

Kem feel up my kep.>

sigh

Okay then, my friend.

Come on. One last time.
For the road.

Come fill up my can.

<Yaaz!
Komm saddelo horzez.>

and call out my men.

<*Zun hook le West Portz.*>

And let us gae free

<*Foriz up wiz bonneto!*

O Bonnez Dundeeeez.>

O Bonnie Dundeeeeeeeeeeee.

<Oh. Byootizful.
Zats ma hame.>.

Your home?

<Dundez. Ayez. Neebor country.>

Dundee? Home?

<Hame.>

I see.

Well, Scotsman. This place is *my* home.

And I did not invite you in.

Come.

Miko.

Please. Don't. I didn't mean
anything by it.

<Zereko kaka.
Vatcheet.>

<Za. Heeren ya.>

Sir. I apologise for
my conduct earlier.

It was most unprofessional.

Please forgive, sir.

Don't worry about it, Miko.
I probably pushed it a wee bit myself.

And it definitely feels weird you
still calling me sir.
Know, after you tried to strangle me and that?

<Yiska ootside.>

<Ja.>

<Vyo?>

<Jaaaaaaa.>

<Draga kalashna.>

Can we maybe…

Can we maybe go?

Now that I've, y'know,
seen your country?

I do not think that would be wise.

Why not?

Outside. There is people.

Oh no.

Is it the paparazzi?

They've tracked me down?

heh heh heh

Yes.

Suppose there are fans out there as well?

They uh.

They know you are here.

You sure?

They ask for the 'Britishman'.

Oh well. So much for being off-duty.
Wonder how Bono copes with this…

Shall we run the gauntlet then?

I will stay in bar.

Few moments.

Aye sure, finish your drink.

Listen. No hard feelings guys, eh?

<Vit?>

I said: no hard feelings?

<Naw.
Scool neebor.>

Hey, if you want to come to the gig tomorrow night.
I'll dedicate a song to youse.

<Zong?>

A song. A SONG.

<Ah vonto songa?
Von lasto teem…

Shya lyav meeee!

Zo I shyeot hoir!>

Ha ha. Quality tune.

<Zat crazy beetcho.>

Might cover it on the next record.

Thinking about a concept album.

About the two sides of me.

Called 'Honey and Banana'.

<Takka zee kyeedz.>

<Takka zee dog!>

C'mon, Miko.

Woof woof.

That dear sweet lady, she leaves me…

<Zo I shyeot haar!>

Ha ha. Okay see ya, guys.
You've been the best crowd of the tour.

But I have a free digital download to promote.

<She lyaaaav me.>

Now open the door. Elvis is ready to leave the building.

<Zo I shyoot hoir!>

RAT A-TAT A-TAT A-TAT A-TAT A-TAT
A-TAT A-TAT A-TAT A-TAT A-TAT A-TAT
A-TAT A-TAT A-TAT A-TAT A-TAT A-TAT
A-TAT A-TAT A-TAT A-TAT A-TAT A-TAT
A-TAT A-TAT A-TAT A-TAT A-TAT A-TAT
A-TAT A-TAT A-TAT A-TAT A-TAT A-TAT
A-TAT A-TAT A-TAT A-

The Pure, The Dead and the Brilliant

By Alan Bissett

Sound of a heartbeat. Soon it is joined by a voice intoning

V.O.   Arbroath   Selkirk   Kirkcaldy   Fraserburgh
Tobermory   Ullapool   Croy   Dunoon
Bothwell   Portree   Brechin   Dunfermline
Hamilton   Rothsea   Stornoway   Strathspey
Larbert   Hawick   Montrose   Leith
Scrabster   Allandale   Falkirk   Alloa

SCENE 1 – A living room in the Faerie Kingdom.
Enter the Bogle, singing an Andy Stewart song – 'Come in, come in, it's nice tay see ye | How's yerself, ye're lookin grand!'

BOGLE   Hiya, pals! Aw, I think we'll need tay do that again. When I say 'Hiya, pals!' youse say, 'Hiya, Bogle!' Okay, yese ready? 'Hiya, pals!' (*audience respond*). That wis mince. Let's try again. 'Hiya, pals!' (*audience respond*). That's better.

Aw, I'm so glad yese could aw make it. I feel like I've no seen yese for ages! Int it just so good when we aw get the gither for a wee dram, a blether and a shoogle aboot? Och, I love Hogmanay. And for any tourists in, that means 'New Year's Eve'. I love the excitement ay waiting for the bells. The chance tay reflect upon the past, the chance tay look furrit tay the future, the chance tay pish in the sink! And for any tourists in, that means 'urinate in one's sink'. Hogmanay is just wannay thay special times on the Scottish calendar. So I would like tay propose a toast. If you could raise your glasses please, ladies and gentlemen, faeries and goblins…to Scotland!

Oh that is the taste ay hame.

And after the bells I've got a special treat for yese aw. Yes, it's… *Braveheart!* Yaaaas!

(*reads from the back of the DVD in American accent*) 'In this stupendous historical saga, Mel Gibson plays William Wallace (*hooray!*), a 13th-century Scotch commoner who unites the clans against the cruel king, Edward Longshanks (*boo!*) This movie resonates long after you have seen it, both for its visual beauty and its powerful story.' (*wipes eye*) Och, I'm sorry, but that film just gets me every time.

Oh here, we're at ten seconds tay the bells everybody! And remember, you have tay wish the people next tay you a Happy New Year okay? That's the spirit ay Hogmanay. Awright, yese ready?

5…4..3..2…1…Happy New Year! (*mass congratulation, then the doorbell goes*) Oh that'll be ma first foot! And for you tourists….ach just work it oot yersels! (*answers the door. Enter Selkie*) Oh, it's you, Selkie! Happy New Year, doll!

SELKIE   Happy New Year, Bogle. I see you're still peely wally.

BOGLE   Aye, it's aw thae deep fried spiders, washed doon wi some Irn Bru. But you are lookin fantastic, hen. Veeeeery glam.

SELKIE   You've got to make the effort at Hogmanay. Is he here yet?

BOGLE   Who?

SELKIE   Em…nobody.

BOGLE   Ooh, I like yer tail. Chic and sleek.

SELKIE   Omega 3 oils. Because I'm worth it.

BOGLE   Whit ye drinkin, hen?

SELKIE   Not for me. I'm off it. New year's resolution.

BOGLE   But it's Hogmanay.

SELKIE   It's those sailors, Bogle. By god, they can drink. Besides,
            I need to watch my figure. I've bloated up over the last
            century. Moving through that water like a bloody killer
            whale.

BOGLE   Dinnay be daft, there's nuthin on ye. Take a drink.

SELKIE   I'd better no.

BOGLE   Take a drink! (*gets audience involved – Take a drink! Take
            a drink!*)

SELKIE   Aye, okay.

BOGLE   There ye go. A nice single malt.

SELKIE   (*sips*) Aw. That is the taste of home.

BOGLE   The best wee country in the world!

SELKIE   Look who it is, Bogle. If it's no a Kelpie. (*coldly*) Think they must *be* something, just cos they've got a bloody great statue of themselves in Falkirk.

BOGLE Och, let it go, you.

SELKIE Kelpie bitch.

BOGLE I dunno whit it is between them. Bloody sectarianism. I've tried tay tell them: nae politics or religion in mixed company. (*door goes*) Oh that'll be another guest! (*opens door, enter Banshee*) Oh hiya, Banshee! Happy New Year!

BANSHEE (*wails*)

BOGLE Och, hen, whit's the matter wi ye? Whit's wrang?

BANSHEE I'm...I'm...I'm just so pleased that it's Hogmanay (*wails*)

BOGLE Well ye dinnay sound it, love.

BANSHEE I've had a terrible time, Bogle.

BOGLE Tell me aw aboot it, petal. Sit yersel doon.

BANSHEE Thanks (*sniff*)

SELKIE Happy New Year, Banshee.

BANSHEE Happy New Year, Selkie. Ye'll be lookin forward tay seein Black Donald?

SELKIE Who?

BOGLE There ye go. A nice wee dram tay warm ye up.

BANSHEE   (*sips*) That is the taste ay hame (*to audience*) Happy New Year, awbody! See? They dinnay even care.

BOGLE   Look, why don't ye just tell me whit's on yer mind, hen?

BANSHEE   Well, if it's no wan hing it's anither, Bogle. Start ay the century there, the pipes burst. Ma cave ended up flooded. Nae insurance. Then ma Mam died.

BOGLE   Whit age wis she?

BANSHEE   Still young. Nine hunner and six. Then ma man left me.

SELKIE   No wonder.

BANSHEE   Just up and left me. Says I'm too dour. (*wails, then suddenly raises glass*) And at this time ay year, awbody, I think we need tay mind oor poor brave boys oot there dyin. They dinnay get tay enjoy Hogmanay.

BOGLE   Um, absolutely (*raises glass*). Selkie?

SELKIE   Whit?

BANSHEE   Oor boys, Selkie.

SELKIE   Em aye. Oor boys. (*raises glass*)

Door goes.

BOGLE   That'll be Black Donald.

SELKIE   Oh, I'm just gonnay go and…oil myself up.

Exit Selkie. Enter Black Donald.

BOGLE   Hello there, Black Donald.

DONALD   *Lord* Black Donald to you, Bogle.

BOGLE   Aye, well it's Hogmanay, so I'm sure we can aw take a day aff. Happy New Year.

DONALD   Haaa! New Year.

BOGLE   Sorry?

DONALD   Haaa! New Year.

BOGLE   Have ye got a fly in yer mooth or sumhin?

DONALD   No, it's just that the word Haaa! is forbidden to a demon.

BOGLE   Whit word? Happy?

BANSHEE Happy! Whit does that feel like?

DONALD   Prince of Darkness, save me from this creature. How are you, Banshee?

BANSHEE Happy New Year, Donald, how's yersel, son?

DONALD   Diabolical.

BANSHEE Still at that whole 'makin the crops fail' racket? Aye, it's good honest work, that.

DONALD   You may not have been out of your cave for a few hundred years, Banshee, but things have changed somewhat from crop failures.

BANSHEE   Oh aye, I heard ye nearly shut down Grangemouth Oil Refinery.

BOGLE   That wis you?

DONALD   Probably getting too old for it, but I've still got to be 'in aboot it'. Such a buzz.

BOGLE   The buzz ay failure?

DONALD   For a demon, Bogle, failure is victory.

BOGLE   Right, well thanks for bringing the pairty, Donald...

DONALD   But there's more to be done. We have to be vigilant about...insurrections. Do you understand me, Bogle?

BOGLE   No really.

DONALD   Scotland. Is not. Safe.

BOGLE   Well, while ye're ruminatin on oor, eh, national security here's a single malt.

DONALD   (*sips*) That's the taste of home.

BOGLE   It sure is.

DONALD   Diagio.

Enter Selkie.

SELKIE   Thought I heard the mellifluous tones ay corruption. Look who it is.

DONALD   Selkie.

SELKIE   Black Donald. I hear you're a Lord now?

DONALD   A just reward for services to the realm. Been working hard since we last saw each other.

SELKIE   And when was that?

DONALD   You tell me. Then again, you never were much good at remembering…dates.

SELKIE   Now now, don't be like that. It's a big sea out there. Plenty fish in it.

BOGLE   Okay everybody, what do we all want from the new year? What are your hopes and dreams? What I want is for the Faerie folk – that's us – to continue to live in harmony with each other and with the people of Scotland. Banshee?

BANSHEE   What I hope for the future is that we never, ever forget the past.

BOGLE   Um, right. Selkie?

BANSHEE   And that I can work through some ay ain personal issues.

BOGLE   Aye, it must be hard for ye, hen. Selkie?

BANSHEE   And that Sidney Devine goes back on tour.

BOGLE   Selkie? What do you want for the new year?

SELKIE   Nothing. I think everything's fine as it is.

BOGLE   Fair do's. Black Donald?

DONALD   I don't care what happens as long as we get it up that fat bastard Alex Salmond.

BOGLE   Oh come on! Yese know the rules. Nay politics or religion in mixed-

DONALD   I'm tellin you, Bogle, if Scotland votes Yes it'll be bad news for us Faeries.

BOGLE   But that's a human hing. Whit in the hell kinda difference does Scottish independence make tay the Faeries?

DONALD   Whit difference does it make? Are you 'aff yer heid'? Put it this way, do you think the people of Scotland could make it work?

BOGLE   Well, I dunno, dae I? I've no got a crystal ball. Wannay thae kelpies stole it and yaized it tay check the shinty scores.

BANSHEE   Thievin bastards.

SELKIE   Shower ay shite.

DONALD   Bogle, you know as well as I do that Scotland is getting a raw deal out of the Union.

BOGLE   Mibbe it is, mibbe it isnay. Who cares, it's Hogmana-

DONALD   It has forever been London's mission to control Scotland. For centuries they used military power, but the Scots proved too tenacious. So they turned instead to politics, bribery. Union.

BOGLE   That's only wan wey ay lookin at it.

SELKIE   Some ay us were there, Bogle.

DONALD   Things that once belonged to the Scottish people later seemed to….disappear.

BOGLE   Whit hings?

BANSHEE   Land.

SELKIE   Waters.

DONALD   Soldiers.

BANSHEE   Oor boys!

DONALD   Oil.

BANSHEE   Industry.

SELKIE   Money.

DONALD   Almost as though *enchantment* had been involved.

SELKIE   Or Faeries….

DONALD   So we need to make sure Scotland votes No.

BOGLE   I dinnay understand. If ye hink Scotland's been getting such a bad deal then why do you want the humans tay vote No?

BANSHEE   He doesnay get it.

SELKIE   Think about it. There's a reason we Faeries still exist.

BOGLE   Whit reason?

DONALD   Scotland is a stunted, terrified nation, Bogle. Every chance it's had to progress it's either shat itself or been sold out by its own.

BOGLE   I dinnay really ken aboot these hings. I just wantay hae a perty, awright?

DONALD   This is why Scotland clings onto its own mythologies.

BANSHEE   It's where it can hide from itself.

SELKIE   That's whit gives us Faeries *life*.

BOGLE   But if Scotland votes Yes?

BANSHEE   Jings! Crivvens! Help ma boab!

DONALD   Well, Bogle, see all this?

SELKIE   Tartan.

BANSHEE   Heather.

DONALD   Braveheart.

SELKIE   Bagpipes.

BANSHEE   Faeries.

DONALD   They're not going to believe in any of that if they're striding forwards intay the future, are they?

SELKIE   Scotland will have become...*real*.

BANSHEE   Too real for us, son.

BOGLE   Oh. I see.

DONALD   Now put a smile on your face, Bogle, it's Hogmanay.

CAST   (*toast*) Slainte!

SCENE 2 – An underground debating chamber.

BOGLE   Thank yese aw for comin at such short notice tay this
emergency congress, but I'm sure yese understand its
importance. Some of yese have come a long wey and the
Parliament of Scottish Faeries would like to recognise oor
delegates from Moray, the Democratic Ghouls; from Fife,
the Anarchist Vampire Collective; from Strathclyde, the
Pixie Workers' Party; and from the Borders, the Trolls
(no heckling please). Apologies from the constituency of
Loch Ness, but our delegate there is solely aquatic and
could not travel. Welcome, everyone.

The subject under discussion is independence
for Scotland, the consequences of this for the Faerie
Kingdom. As you know, Scotland becoming a real
nation will have a disastrous impact on its mythological
creatures.

I call upon our first speaker, from Argyll and Bute,
the Right Hon Baroness Banshee.

BANSHEE   Thank you, the Right Honourable Bogle.

Delegates, friends, I am aware that here in this chamber, many of you may not know how we Banshees sustain ourselves, how we survive.

I will tell you. We feed off misery. It fills our bellies. Our wailing is an expression of our hunger. Our staple diet is that most raw and nourishing of emotions: grief. And so we Banshees seek out death and loss. It wisnay only sheep and landlords that thrived throughout the Highland Clearances. The Banshees feasted.

But two centuries later there came a bounty the like of which we had never experienced. War had begun in Europe and 150,000 Scotsmen, 150,000 of OUR BOYS, gloriously laid down their lives so that Great Britain could protect its Empire. The mourning among the women and children was overwhelming.

And so I call upon this house, this sacred place, to remember that suffering, to remember that the Great War is now one hundred years old. Yes, there have been other imperial adventures for Our Boys, from Suez to Afghanistan, but none brought the same plentiful supply of souls to the Banshees' supper table.

So let us commemorate. Let us never forget. Let the memory of loss haunt every hillside and glen. We must appeal to that sense of servitude. If Scots so are willing to die, then who are we Faeries to protect them?

But also, my fellow Faeries, we need to ensure that suffering continues. We must create a permanent sense of doom, or otherwise WE are doomed. Vote Naw!

BOGLE   Thank you, Baroness Banshee, for that, uh, historical perspective. And please, during the speeches, I'd urge the Shetland Society of Shape-shifters to stick to the one form. Honestly, one minute you're Scots the next you're Vikings. Make up your minds.

Our next speaker represents the seal creatures of the

islands. Please welcome, the Star of the North, the Queen of the Seas, the Fisherman's Friend…the Selkie.

SELKIE   I'm sorry, Baroness Banshee, but that was too depressing. Who wants to hear about death? Who wants to hear about war? Is that what you all came out for tonight? Nooooooo. People want to have a good time, am I right?

Look, everyone. If we want to persuade Scotland, there's no point in bringing them *down*. We need to bring them *up*. Trust me, we selkies have great experience in this field.

Imagine you're a sailor. You're working on the fishing boats, waves crashing all over the deck. You're soaked through to the skin, cold, tired, hungry and you haven't seen a woman in about a fortnight. You look out – and what do you see?

A beautiful female just casually arranging herself around a nearby rock. Just combing her hair, quite the thing, singing herself an innocent wee song. *'Don't you wish your selkie was hot like me…?'* She glances up – Oh, she's topless! And then she sweetly curls a finger, beckoning you forwards, and before you know it….you're up to your neck in brine!

Now, is that gonnay happen if I'm sittin there on that rock spraffing on aboot war and sacrifice? Nobody wants to hear it!

So take it from a selkie: we should be entertainers. That's how you get the crowds in. Ye magic them with glamour and London Fashion Week and Olympic Games Opening Ceremonies. You bewitch the media, you bewitch the people.

I mean, switch on the telly and what would you rather see:

(*solemn*) "Food banks open across Glasgow as living standards plummet"

Or...

BANSHEE   Yes, welcome everyone to The Great British Bake-Off!

BOGLE   Wot's Alfie Moon wivout his Kat?

BANSHEE   And there they are, the Royal couple, William and Kate, smiling there with baby George. Look at them smile!

SELKIE   You understand? We are Faeries. Enchanters. We must use our powers to *seduce* the Scots. So let's not get them thinkin too deeply about war and democracy and the economy and bleugh. The most important question in their minds, when they get into that voting booth, should be: will I still be able to get Eastenders on the telly? Of course they will, but we don't have to *tell* them that! Let's chuck about the words 'Team GB', stick some Union Jacks onto some Top Shop bags, then just Keep Calm and Carry On. It's all under control.

BOGLE   Thank you, Selkie. Isn't she gorgeous?

    Our final speaker of the day is the reason we are all here, the Right Honourable Faerie who tabled the motion against independence. All the way from Faslane Naval Base, Lord Black Donald.

DONALD   With all due respect to my Right Honourable Faerie colleagues, one thing and one thing alone will win this day. History, Baroness Banshee, can be dismissed by those living in the present as simply irrelevant. And seduction, Lady Selkie, is, well, seductive. But it can always be resisted by those with the will to do so.

    There is one emotion, however, which triumphs over all others. A life spent roaming these lands, a cold shadow spread before me, has taught me the value, above all else, of *fear.*

Now, our work is partly done for us. The Scots are a fearful nation, aye wary of the menacing tentacles of the future. They have been bred as nation to feel inferior in status to their Southern counterpart. All we need do is exploit these... insecurities...magnify them, make the Scots believe that nothing better is possible.

Let me give you an example. Bogle!

BOGLE   Yes?

DONALD   The case for Scottish independence, if you please.

BOGLE   Em, well, Scots could make their own decisions about-

DONALD   But the price of oil fluctuates up and down, what are you going to do when it runs out, you can't go crying back to the UK, even although *they've* no idea what *they're* going to do when it runs out, and as for defence against terrorism surely you would be a target for every two-bit bandit in the world without the strength of the Great British security services to defend you. Why...you could be invaded by Ireland.

BOGLE   Aye, but 1 in 5 weans are living in poverty!

DONALD   What's that? Shipbuilding? Well, come on, you know fine well that in the result of a Yes vote Westminster could shut your industry down with one click of the fingers – WE HOPE YOU'RE LISTENING GOVAN – and you wouldn't be able to punch above your weight on the world stage, no-one would care, every time Scotland got up to speak all the other nations of the world would tut and sigh as though you were children wanting a grown-up to see what you've done with crayons. The EU would take one look at Scotland turning up in its trainers and say FUCK OFF! And what currency will you have, oh Sterling is it? Yeah, if we let you. And of course you'd need a passport to get into England, who, by the way, you've abandoned to the Tories, even although that's who they keep voting for.

BOGLE   But why's the life expectancy of a man in Shettleston 14 years below the UK average?

DONALD   Think about those relatives in England. They'd be foreigners. Yes, *foreigners*, cos we all know *foreigners are a bad thing*. You'd certainly never see them because there would a ONE HUNDRED FOOT WALL OF ICE ON THE BORDER LIKE IN GAME OF THRONES all to fulfil Alex Salmond's dream of being Scotland's first ever dictator, cos it's all about him, you know that right? I mean, there's only one person in Scotland who actually wants independence and he's JUST A BIGOT WHO HATES THE ENGLISH.

BOGLE   But if we vote No they could start privatising oor NHS!

DONALD   I mean, don't give me that guff about redistributing wealth and getting rid of nuclear weapons and improving democracy, you just want to round the English up into Gulags and force them to eat kilts and read the poetry of William McGonagall every single day, don't you? No? WELL THAT'S NOT WHAT WE'RE GOING TO TELL THEM!

BANSHEE   But what about Norway-

DONALD   Norway? Norway! Don't make me laugh! Ha ha ha ha. Alright, Norway might have a massive oil fund, full employment and generous pensions but it costs SEVEN POUNDS A PINT. Or is it forty? It doesn't matter, think how much a round is going to skin you. Where's the detail? There's no detail. Detail detail detail detail! Even though every time we ask you for detail you give it to us we're going to pretend you didn't! IT'S AN IMPOSSIBLE TASK, DO YOU HEAR ME? INDEPENDENCE IS JUST NOT FEASIBLE. IT CAN'T BE DONE. IT'S NOT WORTH THE EFFORT. IT'S BEYOND YOUR SIMPLE HAGGIS-STUFFED BRAINS. SAY THESE THINGS LOUD ENOUGH AND FAST ENOUGH AND OFTEN ENOUGH AND NO-ONE WILL BE ANY THE WISER AND THE MEDIA WILL TRANSMIT ALL OF IT FOR US, EVERY SINGLE WORD, BECAUSE WE *OWN* THEM, SO YOU WON'T BE ABLE TO WATCH EASTENDERS EITHER YOU MENTAL! RAVING! HATEFUL! CYBERNAT! MONSTER!

Now, repeat after me.

"Too wee, too poor, too stupid."

(*Gets audience chanting*)

"Too wee, too poor, too stupid."

"Too wee, too poor, too stupid."

You see how easy it is? We've got this won.

Scene 3 – A High Street in Scotland

Bogle and Banshee start handing out leaflets to the audience.

BOGLE   Stop Mad Alex's dictatorship!

BANSHEE   Vote Naw or Nicola Sturgeon will break intay yer hoose and steal yer purse!

BOGLE   Keep Scotland in the Union or JK Rowling will stop writing books!

BANSHEE   Don't break the Queen's heart! She's an auld wifey and she really loves Balmoral!

BOGLE   Price of oil fluctuating as we speak!

BANSHEE   Aye, and I've heard it runs out in about twenty minutes!

BOGLE   Leaflet, madam? Oh, I think we've got a Yes voter here, Banshee.

BANSHEE   Whit? Are you sayin ye want tay live in a Separatist Fascist Tartan Brigadoon?

BOGLE   Is it just cos ye hate the English? Is that whit this is aboot? But that guy brither's English. Dae ye hate him? Oh I bet you dae. Ye've got that mad, mad look in yer eyes.

BOGLE   I despair ay you people. Ye should be ashamed ay yersel. Vote Naw. Or the SNP will eat yer dug!

SCENE 4 – A candelit restaurant in the Faerie Kingdom.

SELKIE   Everything going according to plan?

DONALD   Indeed. Mark my words, Scotland's voting No.

SELKIE   It's good to see you again, Donald.

DONALD   You too, Selkie.

SELKIE   We've had some times, eh? I can still remember the first time I saw you.

DONALD   1603. The Union of the Crowns.

SELKIE   I'd swam with my Mum down to London to see the Coronation of James VI-

DONALD   James I.

SELKIE   James I. Of course. I was so excited. We shook ourselves off on the banks of the Thames, took human form, and she led me through the crowds to Westminster Abbey. Then we went into that vast church to watch the ceremony.

DONALD   There I was.

SELKIE   There you were. Standing at the altar. Next to the throne, yer hand on the shoulder of the new King of England. Ye were resplendent in that beautiful, black silken gown of yours. Black armour shining. Black hair. Black eyes. Black Donald.

DONALD   *Lord* Black Donald.

SELKIE   I thought: if you can make it in London any of us can. When I went back up North, I could just see everything that was wrong with the place. No ambition. I wanted something *better* for Scotland, something to stop us being so...so...

DONALD   So Scottish?

SELKIE   Exactly. You get it.

DONALD   I get it alright.

SELKIE   Made it my business to follow your career after that. Capsizing merchant vessels. Blocking trade routes. Suffocating the economy.

DONALD   A project commonly known as 'The Darien Scheme'. Rather proud of that one.

SELKIE   Watched you at work in 1707.

DONALD   My greatest hit.

SELKIE   Unifying the parliaments.

DONALD   'Unifying'!

SELKIE   Ha ha ha ha! But you know what I mean.

DONALD   I do.

SELKIE   You were in your element. Bribing all the nobles.

DONALD   Again!

SELKIE   Ignoring the democratic wishes of the Scottish people.

DONALD   Don't forget the English people! They didn't want it either.

SELKIE   I'll tell you who wants it.

DONALD   (*growls*)

SELKIE   The way you arranged it so that London got to pick Scotland's negotiators.

DONALD   How silkily I moved troops up to the border. Just in case they didn't get the message…

SELKIE   Masterful.

DONALD   The lies we've told them about the oil!

SELKIE   And they don't even know….

TOGETHER Because we buried the report!

SELKIE   You sexy bastard.

DONALD   (*raising glass*) To the union.

SELKIE   (*clink*) The union.

DONALD   Come here, you minx!

He draws her towards him. She almost lets him kiss her, but stops him.

SELKIE   We've got work to do. You can have me only after Scotland says No. Then we'll have another…union.

Exit Selkie and Donald.

Scene 5 – A High Street in Scotland

Bogle and the Banshee are still handing out leaflets, more miserably now.

BOGLE   Sir? Too wee, too poor, too stupid? Why don't yese all just top yersels, cos nothin's gonnay get any better.

BANSHEE   Your heart's no in this.

BOGLE   Did ye notice?

BANSHEE   Aye, well, ye'd better change yer patter quick. I'm no gettin flushed doon the swanny just cos you fancy a bit of improvisin.

BOGLE   There's just sumhin aboot aw this that doesnay sit right wi me.

BANSHEE   Listen, son, ma last fish supper didnay sit right wi me. Done a jobby. Sorted. Whit's yer problem?

BOGLE   Ach, it's just that I'm a Bogle. An imp. A sprite. We dinnay like bringin folk doon, ken? If I'd wanted tay dae that I'd have been a Ban-

BANSHEE   A Banshee?

BOGLE   A banker.

BANSHEE   (*takes out her phone*) Excuse me. (*rings*).

Enter Black Donald, on the phone.

DONALD   What do you want?

BANSHEE   It's Private Banshee, reportin fae the field, sir.

DONALD   Whit's the matter? Have Yes Scotland turned up? Just stand in front ay their stall tutting and shaking your head. Drives them mental.

BANSHEE   Naw, it's no that. Bogle wants tay talk tay ye. (*hands over the phone*)

DONALD   Bogle? What's the problem?

BOGLE   (*bottles it*) Oh, no problem. Great response here. Everybody hates Salmond. 'There's no detail! Too many unanswered questions!' That sortay thing. It's a No vote. Easy.

DONALD   Excellent. And have you been pushing the Eastenders angle?

BOGLE   Oh aye. When folk hear that they're like, 'Whit? Well. It's Eastenders or nothin for me!'

DONALD   Brilliant. Keep up the good work. There's a special title for you after all this. How about Baron Bogle of Buccleuch?

BOGLE   Sure. That'd be great, thanks. Any last minute canvassin tips?

DONALD   Just keep calling them 'chippy'. Any complaints they have, just say 'Stop being so chippy!' Shuts them right up.

BOGLE   Okay. Thanks for the advice.

DONALD   Do Scotland proud, Bogle.

Bogle hangs up. Exit Donald.

BANSHEE So?

BOGLE Told us to just keep calling them 'chippy'.

BANSHEE Chippy? Aye the Scots are that, awright.

BOGLE (*mutters*) I'm no surprised.

BANSHEE Fair bunch of miserable bastards. Only happy when they're complainin. I mean, look at that yin. Like a dug lickin the pish affay a jaggy nettle.

BOGLE I ken how they feel. I dunno if I'm the mood for campaignin noo.

BANSHEE Get back tay work, you. Mind whit Donald says. We'll aw be extinct wi a Yes vote.

BOGLE But Banshee, mibbe we belong tay the past. Mibbe we've roamed aw the forests and haunted aw the glens that we need tay. These folk could still have a future.

BANSHEE They'll hae a future with or withoot a Yes vote. Point is, we might no.

BOGLE I just wish we could see it.

BANSHEE See whit?

BOGLE The future. Just so we kent exactly whether or no we're daein the right hing.

BANSHEE Och awright, if it'll shut ye up.

BOGLE   Whit ye daein?

BANSHEE   I've got a spell book on ma phone.

BOGLE   Ooh modern, how did ye get that?

BANSHEE   It's the digital version ay ma Mam's spellbook, the same wan that goes right back through generations ay Banshees. Rumour has it, that wis the wan whit made the Stone ay Destiny vanish, and gied the Krankies a career.

BOGLE   Fandabidozi.

BANSEE   Och, I can never cast wi these touch-screen spells. Okay, here goes. 'Witness Future'. That'll gie us the answers. "Teeth of bear and eye of newt / Let us see how things turn oot." (*holds up phone*)

BOGLE   Whit's wrang?

BANSHEE   I cannay get a signal. Oh right, that's it noo.

Enter ORACLE.

ORACLE   Why have you called?

BOGLE   Em, you tell us. Who are ye?

ORACLE   I am the ORACLE 118 118. I see all.

BANSHEE   We wantay find oot whit becomes ay Scotland.

ORACLE   Scotland. Ah yes. That's what the ancients called it.

BOGLE   The ancients?

ORACLE   Yes. You.

BANSHEE   Why, whit do they call it in the future?

ORACLE   They don't call it anything.

BOGLE   How can a country no have a name?

ORACLE   Because it's not a country.

BOGLE   So whit happened tay it?

ORACLE   In 2014 a small, insignificant area of the Northern Hemisphere known as 'Scotland' asked its people if they wanted to leave the United Kingdom. The people voted No.

BOGLE   Oh well, that sorts that oot.

BANSHEE   *Why* did they vote no?

ORACLE   The case was made by a party known at the time as 'Labour' that 'nationalism' was a virus. The Scots believed them, and voted against ruling themselves.

BANSHEE   Ah that's what we wanted.

ORACLE   And so, as the decades passed, people realised there was no need for a Scottish parliament.

BANSHEE   Really?

ORACLE   Therefore a new Greater Britain-

A resonant chord.

ORACLE   – was established. Over time, the place once known as 'Scotland' simply ceased to be. What an inspiring story!

BOGLE   Whit's inspiring aboot it?

ORACLE   Just think about it! Those people, the Scots, making that sacrifice to defeat the *evil* of nationalism and be at *one* with Greater Britain!

The chord again.

BANSHEE   Em, well that depends who wrote yer history book.

ORACLE   There was a word used to describe them at the time...

BOGLE   (*through gritted teeth*) Chippy?

ORACLE   Chippy, yes. Alcoholic. Pessimistic. Fraught with anger. I think, all in all, we're better off without the 'Scots' don't you?

BANSHEE   See while ye're here, could ye tell us whit happens tae the Faeries?

ORACLE   Faeries...? (*scans future*) Yup. Gone.

BOGLE   Ye whit?

ORACLE   Eventually, all the folk tales, songs, stories, languages, customs and poems which made the country distinctive simply...

BOGLE   Disappeared.

ORACLE   Well, if this 'nationalism' was indeed a virus, then the virus had to be cured. All for the good of Greater Britain.

Chord!

ORACLE   Now, do you still need me? Cos, there's a guy from UKIP who wants to hear the good news.

BANSHEE   Aye, awa ye go. Costin me a fortune this.

Exit ORACLE.

BOGLE   So that means if Scotland votes No…

BANSHEE   …the Faeries die?

BOGLE   It's a trap! It's Donald, he's tricked us.

BANSHEE   Dinnay be daft, Bogle, why on earth wid he dae that?

BOGLE   Because he's a *demon*. Dae ye no remember whit he said: 'For a demon, failure is victory.' He *wants* Scotland tay fail. It's whit he's tried tay achieve aw his life and they made him intay a Lord for it. That's why he wants a No vote. He's goin eftir a promotion!

BANSHEE   *(wails)*

Enter Donald, chasing Selkie.

DONALD   What are you pair doing here? You're supposed to be out there canvassing!

BANSHEE   Selkie! He's tryin tae trick us. We've seen the future eftir a No vote and it's pure shite.

SELKIE   But we need a No vote if we're to survive.

BANSHEE   That's the point, hen, we dinnay survive.

SELKIE   What are you talking about? Why not?

BOGLE   Scotland just fades away intay irrelevance. And so do we!

DONALD   They're lying, darling. After all, why would I put you in jeapordy?

BANSHEE   He's at it. Wha kens whit they've promised him for this!

SELKIE   Donald?

DONALD   I knew it! I knew the pair of you would have your heads turned by those poseurs in the Yes campaign.

BOGLE   We've been tellin the Scots a lottay pish, Selkie. Aw tae keep him in ermine furs and champagne.

DONALD   Alright. No more Mister Nice Faerie.

BOGLE   We're no feart ay you.

DONALD   Ha. On my side, I have the full power of the British state, the media *and* the composer James MacMillan.

CAST   Who?

DONALD   Rich people love him, that's all you need to know. What do you two have?

BOGLE   We've got heart and soul!

DONALD   Heart and soul! What's that against the awesome fear of economic collapse? Look at you with your poems. Your actor luvvies. Your meetings in draughty town halls in places like Auchterarder and Tayport. Tired wee people knocking on doors in the rain.

BOGLE   Aye, well, mibbe they 'tired wee people' are whit it's aw aboot!

BANSHEE   Selkie. I ken ye've got a hing for him, and why wid ye no? Tall, dark and handsome, we've aw fell for it. But ask yersel honestly, hen: has he ever made ye happy? Actually happy?

DONALD   And how would you know the meaning of the word Haaaa!

BOGLE   Happy?

DONALD   Moaning endlessly about what's been done to Scotland, what's been done to Our Boys, like a greetin-faced wean. Did ye never think about the weans ay the folk that Our Boys went in there and killed?

BANSHEE   Oh that's no fair.

DONALD   Is it not? The Scots are more like me than you care to admit. I've walked every corner of the globe with them. I was there in India, putting the Hindus to the sword. I was there in South Africa. I was there in old Alabama, forming the KKK. I was there on the slave ships that left Glasgow, full to the brim with weeping negroes. I was there, Banshee. I saw.

BANSHEE   Every country has it's ghosts, son. Mibbe it's time we left the past whaur it is. Even me.

BOGLE   Aye, we can make a different country.

DONALD   Nonsense. I know what Scotland wants.

SELKIE   There's only way to find out what Scotland wants.

BOGLE   How do we dae that?

SELKIE   Let's have the vote right here.

DONALD   Are you serious?

SELKIE   Deadly serious.

DONALD   Ha ha, I don't think Mr Cameron would consider that legally binding, do you?

BANSHEE   I think it's aboot time we had answers.

DONALD   But, Selkie. We might die…

BOGLE   We're no gonnay know whit happens until we take a chance.

SELKIE   Whit's the problem, Donald? Scared of the result?

DONALD   Bring it on. You'll see who this country really belongs to.

SELKIE   Okay, everyone, when you came in you should've been given a sheet with a Yes on one side and a No on the other.

BOGLE   On my signal I want you to show me the Yes side if you're voting Yes.

DONALD   And the No side if you're voting No.

BANSHEE   Okay. Three, two, one…

Let's face it, it's gonnay be a Yes.

BOGLE   It's a Yes!

Bogle and Banshee cheer, but then….lighting change. Thunder-crack. The fairies start to fall sick.

BOGLE   Oh no…

DONALD   You pair of numpties!

BANSHEE   Aaaaghhhh.

DONALD   I tried to warn you!

SELKIE   What's happening?

DONALD   What's happening? We're becoming extinct. Suppose that's what I get for what I did to Rangers.

BOGLE   But I thought this wis gonnay happen wi a No vote?

BANSHEE   Whit went wrang? (*wails*)

The Fairies are on their knees now, moaning, in distress, as though suffering from radiation sickness. But then…they regain strength.

BOGLE   Hang on. Something's happenin. I feel different.

BANSHEE Waaao – Here, whit's happened tay ma wail?

SELKIE Ma skin's drying up. I can't…I can't become a seal.

BOGLE Wait a minute…try and dae magic.

BANSHEE Hand of ape and mouth of troll / Give me the body of a twenty year old. (*beat*) Ach well, worth a try.

BOGLE That must mean…

SELKIE We've become *real*.

DONALD Exactly what I feared would happen.

BANSHEE Part ay the new Scotland.

DONALD Why would you want to lose your powers?

BOGLE Naw. That's cool man. We can actually be involved noo. We would rather have *this* power. The power to change Scotland.

DONALD Oh I'll be involved alright. In the negotiations!

BANSHEE Donald, gie it up, son. Ye've lost.

DONALD No! I'm still in charge. I've always been in charge. I'll always *be* in charge. Come on, Selkie.

Selkie's thinking it through.

DONALD Selkie. Get a move on. Cameron's going to need my help or Salmond will end up owning the Falklands!

SELKIE   That's all this is all about for you, isn't it? Control.

DONALD   Well, of course it's about control. What else is there?

SELKIE   Choice?

DONALD   Come on, Selkie, you promised yourself to me.

SELKIE   Aye, that's the problem. I must've been daft. All those years wasted, pining for you. Lookin up to you.

DONALD   Okay, look, maybe I've taken you a little bit for granted. Perhaps we can come to some new arrangement.

BANSHEE   Whit ye gonnay dae, devolve her some tax-raisin powers?

DONALD   *And* a day off each year for Baby George's birthday?

SELKIE   I'm an independent woman now.

DONALD   Selkie. My love…?

SELKIE   You're on your own, Donald.

DONALD   I see. Well. What options for me now? I could always write a column for *The Daily Mail*, paint a picture for those in the South about this 'new Scotland', stoke up the Caledonian threat hovering on the border, poised to invade Northumberland.

BANSHEE   Donald, come wi us, son.

DONALD   Never. I haven't spent a thousand years sowing discontent in this country to give up now. Not when there's so much false optimism to pierce.

BOGLE   Why does it have tay be false?

DONALD   You'll fuck it up. Scotland, when faced with an open goal, has a habit of kicking it over the bar. So we'll see. You all think I'm the bad guy, the panto villain. But maybe I'll be proven correct, and this is the biggest mistake Scotland will ever make.

BANSHEE That's really saying something.

DONALD   Point is, you won't know I was right until it's too late. Good luck, Scotland. Once the inevitable happens, you'll know where to find me.

SELKIE   Whaur's that?

DONALD   I'll be Peace Envoy to the Middle East.

Exit Donald.

BANSHEE Well that wis quite a year!

SELKIE   A new start right enough.

BOGLE   Feels weird eh? I wunner whit's gonnay happen next.

BANSHEE Aye, that's the excitin part. And it's no gonnay be easy. Sometimes it'll be a hard road.

SELKIE   But if feels like we've walked part of it already.

BOGLE   Aye, then wan day they'll look back on how far they've come, and wunner how it was ever any different. They'll remember...things began quietly – a tut, a sigh, a rolling of the eye – until slowly, scattered, they all came together to do a simple work that mattered: what they were born for.

The pure, the dead and the brilliant hauled themselves back into the world. Flags were unfurled, and people took photographs to show their youth that something mythical had returned. *You.*

You told the truth. You did not cheat. You walked the streets on cold, wet nights, hands tight and numb, knocked on doors, were drummed away by some, but others met you with a smile and a wee 'come in'. *It was really happening.*

Thousands of you filled a hill one summer, thousands of you tired of being lied to, seeking higher ground, coming of age. The world was suddenly your stage. Everything was allowed!

You were not cowed, saw through pretense, did not need to state how 'proud' you were, over and over, defensively. It was evident.

You did not feel the need to be the best, global leaders, world-beaters, just *better.*

You seized your chance. You danced, you sang, you marched, you chanted long into the night, warmed each other up when needed, with a light or a dram or a simple push of the pram. For Auld Lang Syne.

It was time. You were awake. The lights were going on. How could you unlearn what you had learned?

You'd come too far as one shared mood and feeling, yearning for a greater good, a common weal, a *say*, as with one voice, one consciousness, one true belief, one day, we stood up as a people and said YES!

ENDS

The
Moira
Monologues

By Alan Bissett

dugs

– I dinnay gie a FUCK if yer man's a booncer!
Yer dug'll no go near ma dug again. Or ken whit I'll dae? Wantay ken
whit I'll dae tay it?
I'll take its baws and I'll squeeze them like that and see by the end?
It'll look like it's shat oot twa fuckn Pepperami!

And ken whit she says tay me, Babs?
Ken whit that cheeky cow actually says?

> – I'll be phonin the cooncil aboot you,
> Moira Bell!
> I'm sick and tireday your cerry-oan,
> Moira Bell!

And she's jabbn yon bony finger at me like that, Babs

> *jab jab fuckn jab*

I'm like –Ho.
Dinnay be pointn nay fingers at me, bitch.

> – The cooncil! The cooncil!
> *jab jab jab*

– pit that finger doon
or I SWEARTAY GOD hen,
ye'll be wearn it through yer fuckn nose.

Hing is, Babs.
I ken she'll no phone the cooncil. I ken she'll no.
Cos she kens whit she'd git!

Dis she really hink just cos her man's a booncer that means her dug can
dae whit the fuck it likes tay ma dug, Babs? *That whit she hinks?*

TWA YEAR I've hadtay pit up wi this since this pair moved in.

Ma street tay.

(puff)

So then guess wha comes oot?

Aye. Baw Face.

Comes up ahind her and he's like that
PUSHES her oot the road, Babs!

—Whit's the problem here, Moira?

—The problem?
I'll tell ye the problem.
See your dug? Eh, *Petrol* or whitever ye caw it.

—Diesel.

Diesel.

I mean, sortay arsehole caws their dug *Diesel*, Babs?

This cunt actn oot the booncer role right doontay a fuckn T
shaved heid, sovy rings the lot.
I have FARTED harder than he can fight.

—Well.

Darling Diesel, for your information, has been bullyn ma dug.

> —Bullyn your dug?
> That whit this is aw aboot, Moira?
> Even by your standards that's insane.

—Aw is it! Aw *is it!*

Well how come whenever *ma wee Pepe*

goes by *your front door*

Diesel is oot barkn his *rottweiler fuckn heid aff?*

—The day, right,

lets Pepe oot tay dae his business in the gairden

COS HE'S FEARTAY WALK THE STREETS

COSAY YOUR DUG

and Diesel, right,

only comes through ma gate intay ma gairden

and chases *ma wee Pepe*

up ma stair.

UP MA FUCKN STAIR!

Hadtay grab Pepe

lock us in the bathroom

while Diesel stoated in and oot aw the rooms

proberly lay doon oan the duvet and had a snooze

went doonstair poured hissel a drink and watched fuckn *Cash in the Attic!*

And ma sweetheart wis trembln. So whit ye gonnay dae aboot it?

> —Em, whit exactly ye wantn me
> tay dae aboot it?

—I'll tell ye.

I want your dug ROON THERE apologisn tay ma dug.

> —Apologisn tay your dug?
> And how am I meantay make him
> dae that exactly?

—Eh I dinnay ken. Your dug, you trained him, your problem.

…didnay train him very fuckn *well*, I might add…

> —Ken whit, Moira?
> I dinnay even needtay listentay this.

And Babs. Only goestay shut the door in ma face!

Noo.

Babs.

(puff)

You ken me.
You ken I will talk reasonable tay ony cunt.

Til they start shuttn fuckn *doors* in ma face, ken whit I mean!
Sticks ma fit in the door and he's like that
tryin tay brek ma fit!

DOOF.

—Ye've got a problem noo, fucko.

> —Hiy.
> I never invited you in here, Moira.
> Get oot ma hoose afore I phone the polis.

—Phone the polis?
And eh, whit ye gonnay *tell* them exactly?
That yer dug broke intay ma *hoose* and near assaultit me?
That ye just tried tay brek a wummn's fit?

Tell ye whit,
see while ye're there?

(puff)

Why don't ye tell them ye're no even registered at this address?

And Babs, he's like

gasp!

—Ye can *gasp!* aw ye want. I ken the score.
She bootit ye oot twa year ago…and we aw ken whit fur,
by the way…
Somehow ye've sidled yer big fat wey back in.
No sure how, uptay her, her decision,
but ye're aff yer fuckn *heid*, hen.

Ye've no bothered telln the cooncil yet though, have ye?

Nuhhn tay dae wi her mibbe…still claimn Hoosin Benefit?

She's like

—Wha telt you that, Moira?

—Never you fuckn mind wha telt me that!

Cos I'll no land Chelsea next door in it, Babs.
I wid *not* dae that tay her.

Had it hard, her man runnin off wi that *tart* fay the ice-cream van.
Her wi they twa wanes.

And ken whit else she telt me?

(puff)

Says this yin here comes hame on a Setirday night eftir his shift oan the
door, *reekinay* the drink. And he knocks this wummn up and doon the
hoose, Babs. He is a bad bastart. And I'd be dane her a *favour* phonin
the social an gettn him tane aff her and the wanes, ken?

(puff)

I mean, yer hert goes oot.
Ony wummn's wid.

(puff)

But *dis that mean* her dug can take fuckn *liberties* wi ma dug, Babs?

So he kens I mean business noo like, cos he's like

                    —Right, let's jist eh…take a minute here, Moira.
                                        Let's jist calm doon.

—Hey! Hey! I'm calm me, pal! I'm fuckn…Zen!

I'll calm the cunt awright.

                                        —Whit is it ye're wantn?

—Telt ye. Dug. Roon there. Apology. Ma dug. Pronto.

                              —And eftir that ye'll leave us alane?

—Aye.

—And ye'll no be telln nuhhn tay nay social?

—Naw.

—And I've got yer word oan that, Moira?

—Aye. And I wis in the Girl Guides, so ye ken that means sumhn eh?

Disnay laugh likes. Cannay take a fuckn *joke*, this yin.

—Right.
Goan get the dug.

She's like

—Ye're no actually gonnay go *through* wi this,
are ye?

—Hey.
Dae as I fuckn tell ye!

I ken, Babs. I ken.
That's how he talks tay her. In frontay a *neebor*.

Very near pulled him up for it, but eh
we're startn tay make *progress* wi this Deisel cerry-oan and I dinnay
wantay rock any *boats* just yet, ken?

So she goestay get the dug
me and Baw Face is staunin there in the hall and it is *awkward* likes.

(puff)

—Yer hoose is mingin n aw.

(puff)

She comes back wi big Diesel, hinkn he's gon walkies,
so he pits oan this like chain hing? That ken ye yaize tay train dugs wi?
Pits it roon Diesel's neck, he's like

>—Right c'mon, Diesel.
>Let's go and see yer wee pal Pepe.

Wee pal, Babs.
As if a rottweiler's onybody's *pal.*
I mean, ye've seen the sizeay that Diesel, Babs,
he is like a HOARSE
ye could ride this cunt intay battle.
Ye imagine whit a dug that size wid dae tay ma wee Pepe?
Turn him intay a *bathmat*, Babs.

So we heads roontay ma bit. I'm oot the front wi the war face oan. He's
behind wi big Diesel.
She's at the back, tryn tay see whit's gon oan,
obviously wunnern how he's gonnay make big Diesel apologise tay ma
wee Pepe.

(puff)

…truth be telt, Babs, kinday wunnern the same masel…

So we gits roon and there he is. Awwww.
Ken that face he gits when he's waitn for his mammy tay get infay work?

Aye that yin.

Well, he sees big Diesel ahind me?
Boof.
Shites it. Straight up the stair.

—Ye see this? Eh!
See how feart ma dug is ay that bastarday a hing!

Fuckn shair Diesel's no gettn away withoot an apology noo likes.

So I gets up and, Babs, there he is…oan the bed…aw shaky.

—Mammy mammy, dinnay make me!

Like sumhn ootay Watership Down hen.

—Aw ma wee wane.
Mammy'll no let anyhn happen tay ye. But he kens, Babs.

And shair enough we gets back doon the stair and there he is.

Big.

Diesel.

—*Rrrrrrrrrr.*

—Pit yer dug doon in frontay ma dug.

—Ye whit!

Hinkn it's gonnay be fuckn Hungry Hippos time here, Babs.
I pit Pepe doon and this cunt snaps it!

—Oan ye go. He'll be safe.
I guarantee it.

(puff)

—*fff fff fff?*

—*RRRRRRRRR.*

—HO!
DIESEL!
Staaaaaayyy…

—*Fff? Ffff?*

Fff fff ff?

—*rrrrrrrrrrrrrrrrr.*

—Diiieeesel.
Don't you dare.
Don't you touch that dug.
I am warnin you, boy.

—Fff? ffff….

—Diiieeeesel.
Don't. You. Move.

—Hh hh hh.

—Hh hh hh.

—Good boy.

(puff)

Hadtay hand it tay him, Babs.

That is the closest tay a dug apology whit I have ever seen.

—hh hh hh hh.
—hh hh hh hh.

I mean, Diesel looks aboot ready tay buy him a pint or sumhn!

—Telt ye.
Yer dug'll no get nay mair trouble aff ma dug.

—Disnay look like it.

—Sometimes ye've just gottay teach them,
Moira.
The hard wey.

But ken whit?
They always fuckn learn.

(puff)

—Right. Mon you.

And Babs,
I'm no shair if he's talkin tay her or the dug

but they baith shites it.

She hings aboot a wee bit.

—Eh…Moira.
Ye didnay mean whit ye were sayin?
Aboot tellin the social he's still steyin wi me?

—Hen, dae I look like a grass?

Only says that cos he was chuckn the word "polis" aboot, hen.
No ma business whit goes oan in yer hoose.

—Awright. Aye.

But I'm hinkn, Babs.

Hinkn aboot the wey he controlled that dug.

Wan pullay the chain.

How *feartay* him that dug looked. A rottweiler.

(puff)

I mean, widnay be talkin tay me like that ken?
Talktay me like that, he'd end up sniffn ma fuckn erse. But still.
—Ho. Hen.

—Aye, Moira?

—Shouldnay have dangerous animals in yer hoose, hen.
No roon yer wanes.
Ye hear me?

—Em aye, Moira.

—Might hink they're safe. But wannay these days...
He'll *turn*.
And it's yer wanes that'll git it.
And I ken whit I'm talkn aboot here, hen.

—Aye, I hear ye, Moira.

She just drips awa doon the street, Babs
ken

like there's nuhhn else tay say aboot the situation?

(puff)

Here.

Fuckn shair that Diesel willnay touch ma dug again though Babs, eh?

Fuckn *shair* he'll no.

hash

(puff)

(puff puff puff)

fffooooooooo that is gid stuff Babs likes.

That is gid stuff.

Quite *smooth*. Whaur did ye git it? Aye?

Thought he wis still in Polmont.

Aw I mean whit herm? Ih?

They will let durty fuckn paedos roam the streets, hen, but they will lock up an enterprisin young man, just for growin a wee bit hash for his local community? Aw so they can fill the arrest quotas. That is aw it is aboot. And I've gotay go aw the wey tay Bonnybrig for a quarter ounce?

Cannot. Be. Fucked.

(puff)

Cannay get it naywhaur the noo likes. Total desert. Ken wha usually gets it for me? Ken Tony? Babs, ye ken Tony. Works in Somerfield. Tony. Looks like a stoat. Him, aye. Well he usually comes roon oan Thursdays wi a wee bit blaw for the weekend, so we hae a blether, ken, watch the telly, mibbe cook him his tea, jist-

Naw, Babs, naw! Dinnay geez it! Listen, hen, god love ye, yer hert's in the right place. But I dinnay fancy him. I dinnay! Dinnay get me wrang, Tony's a lovely fella. But I'm just seekay men, Babs. Mess wi yer heid, that's aw they dae.

(puff)

I've gottay keep ma heid clear.

Nay offence tae your Graham likes, that's a gid man ye've got there, but I mean, see the restay them? Whit they aw aboot? Aw aye, at the *start* they're brilliant. Dressed up, takin ye oot, peyin for everyhn, geen ye the patter

—Awright, darlin.
Whit's yer favourite Narnia book?

Aye, well I'm the lion
you're the witch
let's find a fuckn wardrobe.

Then fore ye ken it they're breengein in at four in the mornin shit- faced and wantn a shag? No aff me ye'll no! Ken whit Billy says tay me wan time? Tumbles in, reekinay the drink he's like

—Moira...
Moira! Wake up.
Cmon, Moira, ye've no gave me
ma hole for ages.

I mean, Babs. 'Ma hole'.

Kinday cunt yaizes language like that?

I couldnay live wi a man noo, Babs. I'd end up stabbn wannay them. Mibbe quite likin it, ken? Ha ha. Mibbe stab another yin! Pit it up oan YouTube!
Ha ha ha!

That's whit I yaize this stuff for likes. Just stoaps ma heid birlin fur a bit

…calms me doon…

(puff)

Ken sumhn though? Ye've ever noticed it's no the sex ye miss sa much, it's jist somebday tay haud ye at night?

Ma wee Pepe.

There's aw the cuddles I need right there. Eh pal?

Ma wee hairy husband.

Whit's that, Babs? Eh, ye kiddin! Vodka? Wi this? That's whaur oor laddies go wrang, hen! Ken whit they dae, right, Setirday night, they get loadit up oan Buckie, then go roontay Johnny McCall's, *then* they start oan the hash! And they wunner how they aw end up fightn?

Dinnay get me wrang, they're gid fights.

—Buckie! I says tay them. —Laddies ay mine? Buckie!

I mean, it's like fuckn sheep's blood mixed wi Domestos, Babs. Did I no bring them up tay ken howtay take their hash? Kinnay mither am I?

That's the problem wi young yins these days, Babs. They cannay take their drink, they cannay take their hash, they cannay take their fuckn Pepto Bismol.

No like in oor day though, eh? Bottleay Mad Dog 20/20 at the backay the Community Centre. Head intay Fawkurt toon. Awright boys, whaur's the perty? Babs's hoose!

Aye, ye kent whaur ye were wi Mad Dog likes.
The fuckn hoaspital! HA HA HA HA HA HA HA HA HA HA HA HA HA HA HA HA HA HA HA HA HA HA HA HA HA HA HA HA
actually we wur in the hoaspital a few times, that's no funny.

(puff)

Aw it's gid this music eh?

Gid wi a toke. Chills ye oot.

Ken whit this song minds me ay? Billy.
He usedtay like it.

I minds this wan time when he done his bike up, and we went for a run. Uptay Callander, ken oot past Stirling? I'm haudin oan the back. He wis a big guy mind ma Billy, gey sexy in his leathers. *Boof.*

Speed we went.

So we gets there, right, parks the bike, fish supper, bit salt and vinegar, and we just sits there nextay the loch, ken? Jist watchin the sun gon doon. Chilln oot.

And that's when he telt me aboot *her*.

and I hadtay get back oan that bike?

haud ontay him aw the wey backtay Fawkurt?

kennin that?

(puff)

cleanin duties

See these teachers, Babs?
SWEARTAY GOD they are the messiest bastarts oot likes!
I mean, wannay the wanes draps a fuckn Chewit they're straight oan
the case

>—Daniel Watson, is that litter I saw
>you discarding?

'Discarding.' That's how they talk!
But see some ay their desks? Worse than ma laddies!
Newspapers, report cairds, yoghurt pots, banana skins, tissue papers,
orange peels, aipple cores, CHEWITS!
Ye dinnay wantay touch any ay it case there's a fuckn *avalanche*,
they'd find ye twa weeks later!

Ye'd survive that long, Babs. Amount ay food there is lyin aboot.

And as for that staffroom microwave, grease is the *word*.

Clarty. You are right, hen.

Clarty.

Ay some ay them's awright.
Some ay them'll gie ye a wee bit blether in the mornin,
cos they taught yer laddies at the skil.
Well, I say 'taught'.
Steven wis never at the skil.

And Gary? I mean he's ma auldest and I love him hen, ye ken I dae, but
I wis up at that skil every twa weeks for oor Gary.
Every. Twa. Weeks.

—So, Mrs Bell. Let's talk about Gary.
—Em, it's Miss Bell actually.

And ye can see it in their eyes, Babs. Single. Mither.

So see noo?

I make shair tay bum ma laddies uptay them likes,
tell them Steven's got a start doon Grangemooth,
Gary's seein this really nice young lassie.

I mean, they dinnay ken she's fifteen.

Oh here, Babs, there's wannay them I quite fancy…

Charlie…
Charlie Bain…. English teacher.
OH he's braw! Cocky, ken? Confident. I like that in a man. Wee twinkle
in his eye. I mean, a man can laugh me right intay bed, hen.

…usually end up laughin them back oot again, right enough…

Aw the lassies fancy him though.
Like the day, right, staunin ootside havn a fag, Tracey's like

—Oh whit dae ye make ay that Mr Bain in the
English department?
He kin mark ma hamework ony time.

Auld Agnes is like

—Tellin ye, see if I wur twenty year younger

I wid be pullin him like that.

(click)

Or pullin him like *that*, ha ha ha ha.

Sixty two.

—Whit aboot you, Moira?

—Ih? Oh aye, he's no bad. No ma type, ken?

Cos ye dinnay want them steppn up their gemme, ken?

Cos they hink ye're interestit.
Wummn can be like that, Babs. *Competitive.*
Sleekit.

Least fuckn *wannay* them kin be…

Whit dae ye hink I should dae?
Could mibbe like slip a Curly Wurly ontay his desk.
A wee note. 'Hey, Mr Bain, dae ye measure up?'

Ach he's too young for me, hen.
Cannay huv twa cradle-snatchers in the same faimly, no wi the gossip-
merchants roon here.

The day though.

Leanin oan ma mop blethern tay him
he's askn aw aboot ma weekend ken, so I'm like
—Aye me and ma pal Babs, Mr Bain,
we were out at Fawkurt's premier nightspot, The Martell,
or as some folk caws it: The *Tart*ell.
No sure how like cos it's only classy lassies like me and Babs whit go there!

Disnay needtay ken we spent the night oan Bingo.com!
And Babs, he is *lovin* it.

Ken how sometimes wi men ye can jist *tell*
whit ye're danetay them?

Ye can jist feel yersel

reeln them in?

Well ken wha ruins it for me? Posh Drawers.

Oh huv I no telt ye aboot Posh Drawers!
Well.
Works in the same department as him, *obviously* fancies him.
Comes floatn in like this, geen it aw

> —Oh HI, Charlie, hope I'm not interrupting,
> but can we talk about that scheme of work for
> the Third Year? Hi, Moira.

—Hiya.

I mean, fuck's that supposed tay mean, Babs?
'Hi Moira'. Patronisin cow.

Charlie's like

> —Yes, in a second, Julie.
> So Moira, you were saying about your
> weekend. How it did it, uh, how did it all turn
> out with, uh you and these gentlemen?

> —Oh are you swapping weekend stories?
> WELL.

I saw that *marvellous* new production of
Taming of the Shrew at the Citizens Theatre.
Have you seen it, Moira?

(puff)

—I'll wait for the film.

—Ha ha, that is so Moira. Anyway, Charlie, I
was thinking it *might* make a really good trip for
the Third Year, what do you think?

—Oh yeah it's had excellent reviews, hasn't it?
Yeah I think the Third Year would
get a lot out of that.

and that's me OOT.

They start chuckn aboot names ay aw the Shakespeare plays they've
seen. Whit, telly no fuckn gid enough for this pair?

Onywey.

Am I staunin there tae be ignored, Babs?

Am I?

I'll gie ye a wee clue.

Am I *fuck*.

Takes ma mop, heads off roontay clean the Maths corridor.

Wisnay feenished English yet likes.

But fuckn shair I'm no moppn the flair in frontay this posh cow.

asked oot

Aw, Babs, wid ye look at that. 'Judy's Ill, She's Not A Drunk.'

I'll tell ye whit, you take a drink if you want wan, hen.
God knows ye'll need it
married tae that choob.

'My Six Year Marriage Hell.' Six year? That aw? Lucky cow.

Aww. 'My Dog Wants To Be A Fairy'.
Mibbe a wee boyfriend for ye there, Pepe?

Whit's that, Babs?

Naw cannay go oot this weekend, hen.

Cannay dae it likes. Jist got sumhn oan.

Whit?

Babs, I'm no hidin nuhhn!
Whit!

Aye alright listen, dinnay tell naybody, right, cos see if ma laddies wis
tay find oot...

Charlie's takin me oan a date. Naw I'm no kiddn ye!
Aw hings've moved oan a wee bit since then likes.
Have I no telt ye ony ay this?

Valentine's Day, right, thought I'd gie him a wee cerd, jist for a laugh likes, leave it oan his desk. And he's got aw these like posters ay Shakespeare plays oan the waws ay his classroom?

So I went online, looked for like some quotes ken?

(puff)

Couldnay really understand maist ay them, tae be honest wi ye, hen. It's aw 'Forsooth' this and 'Hey nonny no' that, ken like they're aw gay pirates?

I mean, can they no just speak plain fuckn English like us normal cunts talk?

But then I funt this yin. Em how does it go…

> 'Assume a virtue, if you have it not.
> Be great in act as you have been in thought.'

And I thought, *aye.* I quite like that.
Cos at the enday the day, Babs, we're aw aspirin tay be as *great in act* as like we've *been in thought*, ken?
And wi him bein a teacher, *he's* also tryin tay be *great in act.*

(puff)

So I scores oot 'act' and pits 'bed'.

I fuckn did tay!
Well, so whit? Ye've just gottay go for it!
Nay point bein a Wendy Wallflower, waitn for some ither wummn tay come by and tear yer man aff ye!

That'll no be me again, Babs. No eftir Billy it'll no.

I mean, me and him, we just sat aboot smokn hash and watchn the telly ivry night. A wummn ma age shouldnay ken the namesay aw the Police Academy films *in order.*

Police Academy. Their First Assignment. Back in Trainin. Citizens oan Patrol. Assignment Miami Beach. Mission tay Moscow.

That, I think ye'll find, is yer dictionary definition ay a *rut.*

Naw, I'm no sayin it wis ma fault, Babs. She kent Billy was wi me. She *kent* it. And if I see her aboot, I'll punch her face so hard she'll shite it oot her erse likes.

But at the enday the day, if ye stoap makin the effort?
They stoap fancyn ye.

So see noo?

See for this yin?

(puff)

I'm gonnay be the fantasy.
The full fuckn works.

And he'll no get me.

So. The day, right, cleanin the English corridor. Charlie's comin doon this wey, Posh Drawers is comin the ither, he's like

> —Eh, Julie, I was wondering if we could em
> have a word in my classroom for a moment?
>
> —Sure, Charlie, is it about that scheme of work

for the Third Year meh meh meh…

Click.

Noo I just *happens* tay find a spot *right* ootside the door that needs mopped. Gottay dae yer job!

—…*meh meh meh MEH MEH
mehmehmehmeh*

—*MEH MEH meh meh meh MEH…*

—*MEH MEH meh meh meh MEH…*

Door comes flyn open, she's marchn aff doon the corridor like there's a flute band playn. He's like

—Julie, I didn't mean anything by it!
I *wasn't* being presumptious, Julie!

Oh.
Hiya, Moira.

—Awright, Mr Bain.
Looks like ye've got a wee problem there wi Miss Carrell?

—No, it's um. Just.
Y'know. Ach, somebody's given me this silly
wee Valentine's card with a Shakespeare quote
in it that's been, um…
doctored.
It's a bit…saucy.

—(Gasp) Wha would dae such a hing, Mr Bain?

—Well, exactly.
But I thought it was, um, y'know…Julie.

—Why did ye hink that?

—Well, she's the only single woman in the
English department
so uh, y'know…

—It's no only English teachers like Shakespeare.

—Hmph. I think it is actually.
I mean, ha, do you like Shakespeare, Moira?

—Love him.

—Oh.
Um.

(wink)

—Well, uh.
Have you…?

Have you ever thought of…maybe…?
going out to see one of his plays…?
sometime, Moira?

—Got wan in mind likes?

—Well
at the Citizens theatre they're showing
Taming of the Shrew.

Would you like to be

tamed

Moira?

—Hink ye're uptay it likes?

—I'll certainly give it a good go.
How's Friday?

—Friday's fine, Mr Bain.
Friday's fine.

(puff)

—I'll fuck ye, like.

—Is that right?

—I'll fuck ye *hard*.

—Moira…
I'm starting to quite believe it.

I bet you're dirty.

and Babs, I nearly blows it by gon
—*Eh, that's why I'm a cleaner!*

—Aw, I'm right dirty me, likes, Mr Bain.
Aw night though…you're gonnay be wunnern
just *how* dirty.
Aren't ye?

—Well. You could put me out my misery, Moira
and just

                                        tell me now.

—I'll see ye Friday.

And Babs, I just turns,
walks aff doon the corridor,
lets him check oot ma erse.

I have still fuckn got it, hen.

Tellin ye, ivry wummn needs sumhn like that iviry so often,
just tay keep the cobwebs awa,
sumhn tay make ye feel aw like horny and mischievous and

young

(puff)

Whit's that, hen? Oh, I dunno. Wee bit dancin, wee bit drinkn,
backtay his place, see whit happens.

Actually, naw.
Naw.
I'm no drinkn.

I hear whit ye're sayin, hen, coupleay glesses ay wine, relax me an aw
that. But I'd get too relaxed, Babs. Sumdyd say sumhn, I'd pit a fuckn
boatle ower their heid. I'm no wantn him tay see that side ay me.

Well wha kens, he might *wantay* see that side ay me, heh heh….

But *I'm* no wantn tay see that side ay me.

date

The date? The date, Babs!
Aw I'll tell ye how it went. Gets through tay Glesga Queen Street, there
he is

—Moira! I got the tickets.

—Em, I got mine oan the train, Charlie, ye're awright.

—No. For the show.

—Show?

Hinkn, *kinday bar's he takin me tay here?*

—For *The Taming of the Shrew.*

—The Whit ay the Whit?

—The Shakespeare play?
That we agreed to go and see?

Aw.
We're *actually* gontay see Shakespeare.
Oan a Friday night? When the Big Brother eviction's oan!
Naw, we're offtay the *theeata* by fuck. And he's geen it

—Moira, y'know, I just think that's great that
you're seeing *high art f*or yourself.

—Em, well I've got eyes, ken?
Wha else is gonnay see it for me?

         —Exactly.
      That's what I'm always trying to
    tell the kids, Moira. Y'know, this stuff is *out*
  there. It's *for* you. Don't let them tell you it's just
            for snobs.

Can it no just be for snobs? Jist til eftir the eviction?
But then I thought: haud oan a meenit here.

Wha's tay say it's no for us, Babs? I mean, it's written in English. I
can read English. I can even talk it. Oan the phone. Wha's tay say this
Shakespeare's only for folk wi letters eftir their names and big hooses
and aw that, ken? Mibbe it is for the likesay me and you.

Whit did I hinkay it?

Em, PISH.

Maist borin twa oors ay ma life.

Honestly hen, coulda been in fuckn *Norwegian* for aw I ken. And they're
aw like

         —FWAH FWAH FWAH!

And I'm like, dinnay geez it. That's no funny.
So at the end Charlie's up aff his seat.

        —Oh! Wasn't that great?
    I mean, the acting, the staging, the direction!

Only direction I'm wantn's oot!
So oot we gets, and he's like

> —That's how the bard should be done.
> With that kind of passion and commitment.
> What did you think of it, Moira?

—Em… well…I thought it wis really amazn the wey that like the *shrew*
in it…got like em…*tamed*?
Jist did not see that yin comin.

> —Yeah, she's a feisty one, that Kate.
> Bit like you, Moira.

Noo we're talkn.

—So, shall we go backtay yours, Mr Bain?

> —Um. Well, there might be a wee um
> *problem* with that, Moira.

MERRIED.

He is fuckn *merried* and he's no even had the baws tay tell me.

But naw, Babs, naw. It's *worse*.

> —Uh. Well, you see. How can I put this. I, uh,
> I kind of still live with my Mum.

Tell ye this, Babs.
See if ma laddies hink they'll still be steyn wi me
when they are 27 year auld?
I will pit a saddle oan them and I will
ride them right oot that door maself, hen.

—So we'll be gontay Fawkurt then?

                              —Falkirk's not really...on my way.

—Fawkurt then?

Twa oors ay Shakespeare!

                              —Uh, sure. Let's go and
                              check out the uh Falkirk scene.

No a fuckn film set.
So we gets oan the train tay Fawkurt but he will *not shut up* aboot this
Shakespeare cerry-oan. Cos he hinks I love it!

                    —I mean, Moira, I just think it's great that you
                              have that drive and ambition and vision.

Aw gettin a wee bit too Apprentice for me noo like, Babs. Cannay
tell him I dinnay like Shakespeare, case he fuckn fires me.

                         —You obviously don't want to just
                         take in the same crap that they shovel at
                         the masses week in week out. Y'know...Big
                         Brother...reality TV. You're not content to be
                                        just a cleaner.

—Em. Whit dae ye mean 'just' a cleaner?

                         —Well. You're obviously trying to transcend
                              your socio-economic background.
—socio-economic...
Dae ye mean, em

Ye mean, like…me bein fay Fawkurt?

—Exactly.

Hmm. Right. Okay.

—Listen, Charlie. Gonnay answer me sumhn.

—What's that?

—Whit is it aboot aw youse…em, how can I pit this… middle-class cunts that yese have aw gottay *be* sumhn?

—Um. Well.

—Doesn't everyone want to *be* something, Moira?

—I am sumhn.
I'm a cleaner. I'm a mither. I'm pal tay ma pal Babs.
(wink)

—But doesn't everyone want to be something *more*?

—Mair than whit?
How can ye be mair than *yersel*?

I mean, I dunno, Babs. Wis weird, ken? There's Charlie. English teacher. Inspirin aw the wanes n aw that, helpin them pass their exams.

And good lucktay him. I'm oan board wi that. Ma laddies cannay dae that. But I tell ye this:

They are gid laddies.

They walk intay ony pub in Fawkurt, folk's pleased tay see them. They tell a brilliant story, they're gidtay their Mammy, thcy can take care ay themsels, haud their drink. Maistay the time.

Different *kinday* intelligence. Ken whit I mean hen?

See aw that aboot havin tay *be* sumhn? Then be sumhn *mair*. Then proberly be sumhn *mair again*.

I mean, dinnay get me wrang, widnay mind gettin ma kitchen done up. Coupleay weeks in Majorca.

But see as long as I've got a nice baggay grass at the enday the week? That's me. I'm awright.

I mean, whit's he feartay, Babs? Whit they aw sa…*feartay*?

Ken whit? I actually started tay feel a wee bit *sorry* for him.

Int that weird?

(puff)

—Charlie.

—Yeah?

—I dinnay get a night oot very often, pal.
I'm for makin it a late yin, whit dae ye hink?

—Sure. Let's paint Falkirk red.

—Karaoke night in the Scotia bar!

> —Um. Well. I'm not really that big on, uh,
> karaoke.

—Ye dinnay needtay be big oan it. *I'll* be big oan it. You can be wee oan it.

> —Okay. Let's go and uh check out the vibe in
> the Scotia.

So we gets there, Babs, and it is *heavin*. Friday night, ken? And it's Debbie's birthday, so I'd phoned aheid, got them tay order me a cuppla Apple Soorz BAM BAM BAM BAM BAM BAM awright six, and there's Derek and Barry and Kenny, they're aw like

> —Moira! Queen ay the karoake! Geez yer
> Diana Ross!

—Naw naw, I'm no really in the mood, Barry.

> —Ye never heard Moira oan the karaoke? Aw,
> ye'd hink Diana Ross wis in the room
> *wi* the Supremes!

—Nah, just no feelin it the night, Derek.

> —Aw cmon, ivrybdy. Moi-RA!
> Moi-RA! Moi-RA!

Then Charlie's like

> —Will Caesar refuse the crown for a third time?

—Geez that fuckn mike.

And Babs, up I gits. Noo, ye ken I like a wummin that's suffered, me. Diana. Aretha. Nina. Whitney. Britney. Kin feel it *flowin* through me, hen, bubbln up like lava, it's like they're speakn through me. Some cunt near phoned an exorcist. Well there I am, kin feel the hale ay the Scotia lookn at me and I stares right oot at them and I'm like

—STOAP in the naaaaameay love!
Be…fore you brek maaaaaa hert….
Think it ower.

Hoose came doon, hen.
Hoose. Came. Fuckn. Doon.

(puff)

Got a wee *theory* aboot this, Babs. See black folk?
Ken how they aw got like shipped awa fay like Africa and Jamaica tay America and made intay *slaves* n aw that? I mean, Babs, they were folk's *property*. Folk actually owned them. Can ye imagine?

Well. See how cos they never had like a voice in *society*?
I hink their voice wentay intay their music.
That's how it's got that *whoof*. That big Look At Me.
That's how Bob Marley's a righteous dude. That's how it makes ye wantay get up there and belt it oot and feel it move ye, it's got that big I AM, it's got that…*life force*.

You're right, hen.

Well, see oan Friday? In the Scotia? When they were aw…lookn at me?

I felt it.

Life force.

Whit's that, hen? Charlie?

Oh aye, shagged him likes.

He wis shite.

scoatlin gemme

at's it

at's it

Boot it up the park.

AW CMON, YA SHITEBAGS! BOOT THE FUCKN *BAW*.

Long tay go? Twenty seconds? They're gonnay dae it. I *ken* they're gonnay dae it. SHUT IT. They're gonnay dae it.

Cmon SCOT-*LIND*! SCOT-*LIND*! SCOT-*LIND*! SCOT-*LI*

awright, they're no gonnay dae it.

Well, they tried their best. Naw, cmon, Graham. Them laddies are pugglt, look at them.

Went doon fightn, that is the Scoattish wey.

(beep)
Hiya, Mam. Aye, I ken! That's Scoatlin for ye though eh Mam, eywis come *so close*. Ye hink: this will be the time when they actually achieve sumhn, then whit? Pmf.

Aye, ye're right, Mam. Wan goal! That's aw we needed! Wan goal!

Tay bring it back tay 3-1.

Awwww, yese hear that? Says she's been wearin her Scoatlin top aboot the hoose aw day, ivrybdy. And sumhn oan yer bottoms, aye? Cos that wis a helluva fright Tam got when ye answered the door that time, eh?

Whit's that? Aye, oor Gary left ten meenits ago wi it. Just look oot yer door, Mam, he should have the plate in his haunds.

Awright well you enjoy it, Mam. Huv a gid night. Bye.

Right you, Heid the Baw! No talkin tay masel. Doontay yer Gran's wi that dinner, she's starvn.

Dinnay 'Och' me, get movin!

And eh…pick us up twa litres ay Pepsi Max oan the wey back, son. Naw, no Coke or Diet Coke or Coke Zero. PEP. SI. MAX.
And some mixer. Aye, Smirnoff.

And dinnay be geen them pakis nay cheek this time!

Honestly, Babs, see the cheek he geez them pakis? Sometimes I worry that boy is growin intay a racist.

Well, that is it. Gemme ower.

But we let them ken they'd been in a fight, Graham! That is the Scoatish wey. That's the spirit we yaized tay stuff the English in them famous battles.
The Battle ay Bannockburn. The Battle ay Stirling Castle.
That ither yin. Whit wis proberly in Braveheart.

Culloden.
If Scoattish history has taught us onyhn, Graham, it's that there's *always another chance*

tay get shafted.

Whit's he sayin noo, Babs?

Graham, whit exactly d'ye mean 'We'd have won that gemme if we were an independent nation'?

Dinnay you start wi yer politics and religion cerry-oan! No at a perty.

But see while ye're at it. Whit does that even mean? 'Independence'? We're aw fuckn independent.

I'm me! you're you! she's her! he's him!

Ye dae yer ain hing. Sumdy gets in yer road, ye burst them. There's ma politics right there. Debate that wan in the Hoose ay Lords.

Wey I see it, we've mair in common wi ordinary cunts in Liverpool, Nottingham, Manchester, Leeds, Newcastle than we have wi these rich bastards through in Embra, Graham.

Royal Bankay Scoatlin, pal? Whaur they fay?
Embra. Fannies.

At the enday the day, we are aw Scoatlin supporters the gither awready. Iviry single wannay us is Jock Tamson's bairn, proud and true and ready tay stand united under the wan-

Partfay the Catholics, aye.

Support Republic ay Ireland first, the cheeky cunts.

But apart fay the Papes, we are aw Scoattish people united and-

The Huns tay, ye're right, son. Ye'll no get nae bigotry oot Moira Bell.

Their Rid Hands ay Ulster. Way backtay Ulster and fly them, ya shaven-heided fuckwit.

But partfay the Papes and the Huns we are aw Scots through and thr-

Aye, let's no forget the Muslims!

Drivin flamin jeeps intay airports fullay Scoattish cunts just wantn their twa weeks peace in Majorca!
Take the ninja mask aff yer wife's face, then we'll talk.

But partfay the Papes, the Huns and the Muslims, we are aw united under the wan-

And the paedophiles, Babs, goes withoot sayin. Obviously. They arenay even fuckn *human*, never mind Scoattish.

And ken wha is the lowest aye the low?
See these Scots that go ontay Big Brother? Embarrassn themsels and the hale Scoattish nation? I mean, how is it nearly iviry Scot whit's been oan that show has been a bawbag?

Federico.
Yon ginger cunt fae Hamilton wi the biceps. That…cat-man. In the leotard. Lap lap lap.

Ken Livingstone, aye *him*.

So. Tay recap! Partfay the Papes, the Huns, the Muslims, the durty fuckin paedos, aw them arseholes that go ontay Big Brother embarrassn themsels and the hale Scoattish nation *and ivrybody in Embra* we are aw Jock Tamson's bairns, Graham.

So I will have *nay* politics or religion in this hoose, thank you very much! Aw we've got a perty gon noo, eh. Onybody wantay debate onyhn else?

Fucksakes.

Let's lighten hings up a wee bit eh? Wee song. Cmon son? Naw? Babs, dae yer Girls Aloud? Somethn kinda ooh…?

Jumpn oan ma toot-toot…?

Graham? Johnny Cash? Johnny Nae Cash?

Whit aboot 'Goodbye Horse'? Aw cmon.

> Goodbye hoooooorse, goodbye hooooooorse,
> I was saying goodbye to my hoooooorse,
> And as I was saying goodbye to hooooooorse,
> I was saying goodbye to my-

Aw fuck yese.

Needtay be another solo effort fay Moira Bell then! Noo. Graham. Ye ken ma faither wis a songwriter?
Aw aye, Fawkurt's ain Boab Dylan, that's whit they cawed him. He wrote 'Goodbye Horse'! Mair proof dae ye need?

Ho. Peanut Heid. Aff that phone. Yer grandfaither's song.

> In Glasgow's fair city, there's bags ay hotels,
> Who offer their lodgings tay aw the big swells,
> But the best wan among them remains tay be seen.
> It's the beautiful building controlled by our Queen.
>
> So first ye gang in, and they ask ye yer name,
> Yer age, yer address, and the reason ye came.
> Noo after these questions, the screw rings a bell,

And he orders yer bath in Barlinnie Hotel.

So after your bath, you're dressed up like a doll,
Wi a jaiket and troosers and a number and all,
Ye go intay yer bedroom, one helluva smell!
Be ye can't pick and choose in Barlinnie Hotel.

For there's bars on the windays and bars on the door,
And a wee widden bed not one inch from the floor.
And the reason I tell ye…I've been there masel.
So I'll recommend youse tay Barlinnie Hotel.

Now the day it has come for me tay depart.
I'm as sick as a dog but there's joy in my heart.
And for aw these great comforts, I'll truthfully tell:
I'm no comin backtay Barlinnie Hotel.

Tara-dee… Tara-dee….
Naw, I'm no comin backtay Barlinnie Hotel.

(puff)

Aye.

Ma Daddy.

And Babs, see when I wis a wee lassie? Visitn him? In Barlinnie?

That's the song I took awa wi me.

That's whit got me through.

(puff)

Pepe?

C'mere the noo, darlin.

Come up and gie yer auld Mammy a cuddle, eh. She needs it, pal.

Aw he likes you, Graham.

(puff)

Ken whit, I might just let big Diesel have a go at you the next time. Could be dane wi a new bathmat.

Graham? Ho. Ye listenin, pal?
Ho, Graham.

YOU TAKE GOOD CARE AY MA PAL BABS, AWRIGHT.

NAW, YOU TAKE CARE AY THAT LASSIE.

Cos she is one in a million.

…I wis won in a fuckn raffle…

Naw, I'm awright, I'm awright.

Whit's that?

England gemme?

Ho. Turn that telly up. Wha's got the remote?

So…

if they miss this penalty they're oot?

Right we've got a game oan noo, eh! Here we go!

He's gonnay score it. He's gonnay score it. England are jammy like that. I ken he's gonnay score it. Watch this.

right wheesht wheesht here he goes

He's missed it!

Fuckin YAAAS! Whoo! Whoo! Whoo!

Oh floweray SCOT-LIND! When will we seeeeeeeee yer likes agAAAAAIN!

Aw that has cheered me right up noo likes! Ye hane that, Graham? Ih?

Ken whit? Scoatlin might let ye doon. But England never dae!

heh heh

(puff)

Here, Babs. C'mere.
Mind yon time we went doontay England for the weekend?

Blackpool. Long ago wis that?

Aye? Fourteen year? Whoof.
Four. Teen. Year.

Aw that wis a gid weekend though eh? Mind we had a drink oan the train
oan the wey doon, whit wis it? Peach schnapps. Aye, and Kestrel. And
we met that stag perty, beat them at pool n aw that.
They had yon daft accent, whaur wi they fay? Yorkshire! That wis it.

> —Where was it you said you were from then,
> Moira?

> Falkirk?

—Eh, it's pronounced 'Fawkurt'.
Speak the Queen's English, pal.

Mind that braw wan wi the hair? Flirted wi me a wee bit.

> —So, Moira, I don't see a ring on yer finger.
> You married?

And mind whit you said tay him?

No mind, Babs!

Ye said

> —Aye.
> She's merried tay me.

Well, here we are, hen. Fourteen year later.
Still merried.

(wink)

Whaur is that boy wi that vodka?

Here, Babs. See oot there?

Fawkurt.

Awright, Fawkurt?

Ye ever look at this place, Babs?

Naw I ken ye look at it ivry day, but I mean look like...*intay* it.

Right, whit am I tryn tay say?

Mind them Magic Eye pictures?
We were in the chippy yon time, waitn for oor fish suppers, and there wis this hing oan the waw, jist like this jumble ay shapes and colours and ye stare at it like that...aw cross-eyed...and ye stare and ye stare and then...

It goes 3-D.

Oh I dunno, a dinosaur or sumhn. But whit I'm sayin is

Ye walk aboot this place aw day and there it is. Same folk, same faces, same buildns, same same same. It's jist Fawkurt. But if ye look at it for long enough....

It goes 3-D.

Ken there was a time I thought aboot movin fay here.
Aye hen, didnay tell ye, didnay wantay worry ye. It wis eftir me and Billy split up, jist thought fuck it. I'm oot. Jist wantit tay get right ower the other side ay the world, ken.

So got the train through tay Embra.

Ended up at the zoo.

Och I dunno, jist wantit tay see aw the wee animals, ken, their funny faces n that stoned obviously

but I minds this…polar bear enclosure.

Fake icebergs. Fake snaw. Fake pool.

And there's this polar bear jist…lyin there.

And it's fur's aw matted and its teeth are yella and its claws are aw rotted.

Jist looked…depressed.

Noo these things are fearsome, Babs. Mind them oan that Lonely Blue Planet Earth hing? Boof. Take yer heid aff wi wan paw.

And there it wis. Fuckt.

And I thought: that is whit happens when ye take a big, beautiful, magnificent beast like that ootay its natural environment, and ye stick it doon

in Embra.

(puff)

So ken whit, hen?

I'm fine whaur I am.

I'm fine whaur I am.

The Red Hourglass

By Alan Bissett

Housebound

We are a proud and ancient race.

We first appeared on this earth 386 million years ago, evolvin tay adapt tay oor environment, learnin trades as we went. Some ay us are simple weavers. Some dig tunnels. Some are highly potent chemists. Some ay us are the architects ay great, complex edifices that make yer Forth Bridge seem puny.

We are hunters.

Yese hate us.

We live in the shadows whaur its warm and damp. This suits a sensibility which might best be described as, heh, gothic. We creep intay yer hooses and ower yer skin while yese sleep at night and we can even get intay the cots ay yer babies.

Dinnay lie there wi yer mooth open.

This is oor world: quiet, quiverin, sensitive tay every vibration, every twitch ay oor prey. For each wannay youse on this earth? There is one thousand ay us.

But still yese think yese have got the right tay dictate terms?

'I dinnay like the wey they move, why dae they havetay move like that!'

Let me tell ye somethin. We dinnay have tay move like that. We just dae it tay wind up the arachnophobes.

'I dinnay like how fast they scuttle across the flair!'

Speed is everythin tay a predator.

'I dinnay like their eyes. Why dae they have tay have so many eyes?'

Well, dearest humanity, youse are the wans presently daein aw the lookin. That's what ye've got us in here for...

I suppose we dae go back a long wey the gither though eh. Faither telt me this story wance, says that hunners ay years ago, right, wan ay oor ancestors is in this cave in the Highlands, tryin tay build his web. No happenin for him. Wind keeps blawin it in. Builds it again. Same hing happens. It's like he's no got the tools or the wits, like aw his trainin's deserted him. And again. And again. Been at it for days, and he's starvin, and the flies are stoatin past him like: Get it right up ye!

Then in walks this guy. Kilt. Sword. Face like a well skelpt erse. And he's like, 'Wee man! I am Robert the Bruce, King of Scotland. We are takin a pure hammerin aff the English and I am just aboot scunnered.'
(I'm paraphrasin, obviously)
'I am hidin in this cave so the English willnay find me, and I am right captivated by your epic struggle tay build yon web. Watchin you tryin and failin and tryin again has made me wantay get back oot there and stove their greedy, imperialist heids aw the wey in.'
'Gon yersel,' says the spider, 'Get stuck right intay them.'
'I will!' goes the Bruce, and awa he goes, and the spider hears the glens ring wi steel. And so, takin heart fay the Bruce's struggle, he finally completes his web. Then the invaders, baith insect and human, die some truly horrible deaths...

Speakin ay which. Need tay talk tay yese aboot Afghanistan.

Noo. There's a certain type ay us has evolved tay survive in the harsh desert environment, and until yer – *cough* – wee incursion nay western man even kent they existed. They're huge. Hairless. White as bone. They play this game wi the sojers. These spiders like the shade, so whenever they find somethin in the desert whit casts a long, cool shadow across the sand – like, say, a human being – they scuttle towards it. When the sojers see the spiders comin they run, hinkin they're bein chased. The spiders run eftir the shadow, and when they're agitated like this they make this sound that goes eeeeeeeeeeeeeeeeeeeeeeeeeeeee!

Heh heh. Personally, I hink they're just puttin that oan.

But when we hear these stories aboot oor Afghani brothers and sisters we laugh, imaginin the fear ay these men, chased by screamin, skeletal horrors. Grown men. Sojers. Runnin for their lives? Fay wannay us? Fuckin brilliant.

Scuse me. Hostin duties.

Awright, mate, no seen yer face afore, how ye doing-

Hiy hiy hiy it's cool, gadgie, I'm no gonnay hurt ye! Here we go again...

I ken I ken, ye dunno whaur ye are. Gie yersel a couple ay seconds and calm doon. Whaur d'ye come fae?

Where. Do. You. Come. From.

Venezuela! Fuck, that is far. Hoat in that jungle? Lucky bastard.

Well ye're in Scotland noo, bud, better get usedtay it. Whaur the sky is blue and so is human skin, heh heh.

Let me guess – ye cannay mind a hing. The auld wavin a bittay gress trick, make ye hink it's food, then huckled straight intay the jar? That's how they get ye, ma man: manipulation and deceit. Same story wi every gadge in here. Saying that, em, the wan that got me? Nay lures, nay fumes – stuck his finger oot and I crawled ontay it. That's what we get for trustin them eh.

Whit's that? Aw aye, shoulda said, ye're in the Reseach Institute. In St Andrews. I ken that's no technically Scotland...

Beats me whit they want us for, pal. Aw I ken is every so often some ay us get tane oot, ithers get pit in.

I hink they're takin bets.

Affects everybody different though eh. See that recluse spider? See when they first brought him in here? Ran aboot for three hours tryin tay find somewhaur tay hide. Kept talkin aboot fuckin...scorpions!

Can I ask you somethin, pal? Are you a tarantula?

Aw, I *thought* it wis wannay youse. Always wanted tay meet wan eh. Well, yese have been in that many films.

Em, dae ye mind if... D'ye mind if I hae a wee look at yer fangs?

Just go intay yer attack position there...like that...aye...

Oh ya bastard. Look at the size ay them. They're like *curved* and everyhin. Nay fucker in that jungle messin wi you eh?

Aye, yer pedipalps are some size an aw. Ooft. Kinday like throbbin, mate. Nice and big. Ye must have a lottay sperm in there. Bet the lassie spiders love you, oh aye I bet they dae....Can I just...have a wee....feel ay them...

Cheers.

Been locked up in this tank for too long ken? Ye get a bit...frustrated. Mibbe me and you can, eh, *take care* ay each other eh.

Yese get a good look at that aye oot there, aye? Perverts. They like tay watch.

Psst! Wee health and safety tip. See Her Majesty there? Stey awa fay her. Aye, I ken she's gorgeous, that's the point. See that red hourglass on her belly? That's the sign ay a black widow, mate. Psychopath. Wan hing squarin uptay me, but she'll fuck ye up, tarantula or nay tarantula.

No that she acknowledges us onywey, the snobby bitch. Proberly just doesnay wantay share a cell wi the rest ay us gadges. Wha can blame her eh?

Hing oan. Ye hear that? Shhh. Stey still. Shhh.....

bzzzzzzzzzzzzzzzzzzzzzzzzzzzzzzzzzz

Fuck ye!

Heh heh. I've still got it.

Aw that's gid. Fresh. Bluebottle. Cannay beat it. That'd go nice wi some Irn Bru, tellin ye. Tuck in, bud, there's plenty left.

Aw right, ye prefer birds. Fuckin show aff...

At least against the insects it's a straight fight eh. Evolution's likesay bred us intay that predator-prey dynamic, ken? Flies can fly, we build webs. Thay human gadges though? Twa hundred times the size us, and they've got us locked up in a tank? Naw. That's just bullyin.

I mean, look at them. Ugly bastards. We've got tay eat in frontay them. Sleep. Shag. Shite. Nae privacy. Nae peace. I mean, mate, I'm a hoose spider. Does this look like a fuckin hoose tay you?

Whit yese got us in here for eh?

Is it jealousy? Yese envious ay oor fine silk threads? Oor speed? Oor reflexes?

Or is it cos we appear in yer nightmares? And ye've gottay *humiliate* us like this.

So if we're lucky ye'll catch us and chuck us oot the winday. If we're no? Ye'll stamp oan us. Or pull oor legs aff. Or experiment oan us.

Aye, ken whit? That's exactly whit it is, mate.

It's fear.

Reclusive

Who the hell are you! Stay back! Don't come any closer!

Uh. I'm still in here?

Say, why don't you people stop looking at us all the time huh? It's kinda creepy, I'm just saying.

I see the boys have got the, uh, fly carcass there, well, uh, yeah, I guess I'm kinda hungry. C'mon, fella, just talk to em, just go up and *talk* to em, man-

No I can't do that, I can't *do* that.

Is that a tarantula? Aw, that's great, that's just fucking great, man. Look at the size of that bastard. I'm gonna wind up dead before morning! They are great hunters, man, I mean the best. All that stalking and running, it's really very impressive – I live in a hole. Essentially, yeah, I live in a hole. Something goes past I'll take a look, but, uh, I keep myself to myself, y'know. I'm a stay-at-home kinda guy. Like, the uh little Scotch fella over there? The house spider? Well, I'm a, I'm a, I'm a recluse spider. Okay, I said it! I like my own company, that okay with you?

Yeah, I mean, we're very, very venomous! And we can be aggressive if we're trapped or cornered, y'know, but, uh, I don't like to talk about that. It's my family, it's not me. I get very nervous in conflict situations. I just wanna be a good father and husband to my wife and the boys.

Aw gee, I sure do miss em, lemme tell ya. I worry about her. How she's gonna cope with those three thousand kids, man? But I worry about everything. Overpopulation, insect shortages, web-building regulations – the political stuff, y'know?

I worry about the lady over there too, with the, uh, red hourglass? She's a widow, y'know, she's probably very lonely.

Yeah, I know how that feels.

How long's she been here, weeks? I mean, god knows everyone takes a while to adjust, but at some point it's like sink or swim, y'know? And I gotta tell ya, I think she's sinking. I really do. Ain't that a shame? Beautiful lady like that? You ask the little Scotch fella, he reckons she's a psychopath.

Nah, man, she ain't no psychopath. Psychopath can't feel remorse.

I mean, rumour has it, she volunteered for this place. Can you believe that? She bit a human being – a little girl – and she didn't even run, man, I mean she just gave herself up. She *wants* to be here. There is somethin very sad about that, right?

All the same, y'know, I'm keepin an eye on her! I mean I sympathise with the broad, but I gotta watch my back in here. We dunno what you people are gonna throw in here. What you got for us, huh, a scorpion? You got fucking scorpions coming in here?

Scorpions, man, jeez, I hate em. They got so many goddam weapons! You ever fought one? I live in the corner of this garage out in Brooklyn. This goddam scorpion just walks right the fuck in, and my wife she's like, 'You better do something about this!' Aw jeez. So I'm like, 'Buddy! You better, uh, get the hell outta here!' 'What you gonna do about it?' Asshole. These bastards is fast, man. You can't move for those, uh, what are they called? The pincers, yeah. And this tail is, like, jabbing at you! But hey. He's forgetting something, man. I'm a goddam arachnid! Come on, you *fuck*. Yeah! Yeah! Faster than you! Bring it on, man! You know who you fucking with? Huh? Do ya?

Kicked the shit outta me, man.

So don't you be bringing no goddam scorpions in here with us, okay?

Hey. Hey. You people even listening to me?

C'mon lemme out just for second. Lemme outta here. Come on, man! I mean, I'm a recluse spider. There's nowhere here to...*reclude*.

You don't need me.

It really is the lady you're interested in, yeah? I mean for crying out loud – she's a black widow! That is a very, very dangerous spider. What's a recluse spider to you? I'm just a joe. I mean, I can barely produce silk. My eyesight is very poor. What use am I to fucking...science, man?

You're gonna let me go. Huh?

Yeah. Well. You just think yourself lucky I'm on my own, man.

If the conditions are right, we recluse spiders? We swarm. Yeah. We swarm together, like bees or ants or something, a fucking *army* of us, man. Too many to kill, even for you bastards.

I remember this one time, we sneaked inta this broad's apartment, y'know, up on Queens? I mean, just high jinks, we wasn't gonna, like, *kill* her or nothing. Although we could. If we wanted to. It was just the thrill of the thing, y'know, running with the gang?

Anyway, we stayed there for quite some time. It was a good pad. It was warm, there was plentya cockroaches, and we found this real nice spot, under the bed? Only thing was every other night we had ta listen ta this broad banging her boyfriend, y'know? And my friend Lenny – from the Bronx – he says 'hey, I dare ya to go up there!' I says, 'Lenny!' I says, 'I wouldn't last two mintues up there, man, with them rolling around and the bed shaking and all?' I mean we was barely hanging on. 'Nah man,' he says, 'I gotta see how this species does it.'

Lemme spare ya the details, it's disgusting.

'You go.' 'No, you go!' 'You scared?' 'Naw, I ain't scared; I'm just a recluse spider, man! Clue's in the fucking name!' 'Okay, I'll go.'

Up he goes.

So what happens? Broad lays eyes on him. Screams! Next thing, y'know, the mattress is overturned, boyfriend's standing there with a broom, it was really quite a scene; she's tearing her lungs out and this guy is slapping at us, and we scatter in like ten different directions, it was fucking hilarious, man.

They they calls the exterminator.

Comes in, picks me up, puts me in a glass box. Goes to work on the room.

They use this chemical. Works on a spider's central nervous system, y'know, shit starts breaking down in there. Sprays the whole floor with it. And I'm in this glass container. Watching this. Watching em die. My brothers. They was trying to get out the room, they couldn't get out the room, their brains is turning ta mush...

So they turn on each other.

Whole swarm. Fangs bared. You got spiders on their backs, kicking at life, as other spiders sink their fangs inna them, man?

Arachnid-on-arachnid violence.

Admit it. You love it. I mean you get off on that shit. You make fucking TV shows about it. You wanna watch us rolling around on the floor together, so you can tick that box that says 'aggressive species'.

And you bring me here. For whatever. And I'm the lucky one?

Yeah, I'm a real recluse now.

This is what I've learned, man: Humanity. Always. Wins.

So if it's okay with you? I'd just like to go home to my wife and my kids.

Hairy

I am tarantula!

I am te largest arachnid in te world. I kill lizard, rodent, bat and of course te bird. I am Goliat Birdeater. Big and hairy. I am te i size of te plate from which you eat your dinner. I was even in a movie! *Gigantic Arachnid Trez.* I am te i spider you tink about when you tink about te i spider. Not tese petty creature tat can only kill cock-a-roach! Heh heh. Tis 'recluse i spider'? Why is he hiding? What has he to be ashamed of? He is i spider! And te 'house i spider'? A i spider does not belong in te house. We belong in te jungle!

In my country? I am worshipped.

Te Piaroa tribe of i Southern Venezuela? Tey eat tarantula. It is part of te i ceremony, tey want to consume our i soul.

Tey lure us out from our hole with a piece of grass, then place two finger on our back, fold up our leg,s tie them in a bunch and carry us back to te camp. We are i stabbed, we die, ten we are cooked and eaten.

Noting is wasted. Even our fangs at te end of te meal? Tey are used as toot-pick.

And yet none of tis tribe has ever been bitten by one of us.
You know why? We lerr it go.

Tey respect us. Tis te greatest honour for tarantula warrior: to be killed and eaten by tese hunter. We prepare for tis fate from when we are little i spiderling. And I know tat when it is my time to be taken to te Piaroa village, it will be where my fater and my fater's fater were i slain, and where teir exoskeleton i still commune with te jungle.

But you people? Tere is no respect.

You are not god. One bite from te lady in te corner would make you tink again. Two bites? You would kneel before her. If you could kneel. Because your leg would have witered away!

So I come to your country and you laugh at me?

You know how important i strength is to te tarantula? It is everyting. We are gladiator. Warrior. Glorious! Fighting! We take control of our jungle. We patrol. Even te i snake fear us!

Tere is only one insect who can make te tarantula its prey.

Te hawk wasp.

She hunt te great arachnid through te jungle of i South America, and when i she find us i she dance before us, hypnotising us.

So beaurriful. Entrancing. Such a creature i she just–

i she make you–

...i so pretty...

hello, pretty

Ten while we are dazed like tis? She walk between the i spider's leg, underneat our fang, and i sting us. Right here.

But we do not die. Oh no.

Te wasp lays her eggs in te i spider's abdomen. Te tarantula is the incubation chamber for tis *bastardo*. Te grub, when it hatch? It gnaw trough te eggs ten feast on te i spider.

All of tis while we are i still alive.

Tis is the arachnid holocaust, te darkest story in our culture. It inhabit our race memory. Each of us can feel te tousand bites of the infant wasp, can feel our flesh being emptied, turn into te dry husk, while tey proliferate, laughing at us for our powerlessless!

We take out tis hatred on all of insect kind. Dragonfly! Cock-a-roach! Mot! Locust! We do not discriminate! We despise every i single one of tem! Our race's impotence against te hawk wasp burns witin us and as one i species we promise tis:

Wharrever walk on i six legs will die. Painfully.

Tis is i something which i suspect te lady? She know all about.

She is a black widow i spider. She very, very dangerous to you, no?

But she is so i sad. I wunner what has happened to her?

She is so i small and delicate. Her beaurriful leg. Tey look like tey could break. She is like a black jewel. Tat red hourglass flashing at me.

I want her to come to me. I want to protect her. I want to hold her in my arms, and tell her that everting? It will be alright. I do not care what i she has done. We are i spiders. Togeter. Far from home. I want to her crawl upon me. I will take care of her.

But perhaps tis lady do not need protection from a tarantula. Perhaps a tarantula will need protection from te lady, eh?

Do not think we will forget tis indignity you have done to us.

One day, you know, we i spider? We will take you all by i surprise. You will be i safe at home in your beds? And we will crawl as one, and kill you where you lay.

An uprising!

A revolution!

One day, my friends, tere will be no wall of glass i separating us.

Widowed

This is what you do. You prepare yourself. Slip on those thin, black stockings, and let me tell ya, I got great legs. You polish your abdomen til it glistens. Then last, you paint on that red hourglass that tells everything that ain't a spider it best be careful. But tells the boys... come take another look.

Well hello there, sugah. You sure do look mighty fine this evening, big ole handsome fella like you? You gonna take a lady out and treat her properly? I mean– I can *trust* ya?

We exchange signals to establish that we are of the same species.

Bow. Curtsey.

He'll weave a web on the ground like a blanket being laid before a lady. How charming! Gentleman will then rub his abdomen on the surface of this web and in so doing release a quantity of semen. Mmmmm. Using his pedipalps – those are the appendages between the fangs and forelegs, y'understand – he will absorb the semen til they are full and thick.

Then he plucks at my web like he's playing a harp, stroking the strands of my silk, and I will show my appreciation for this by raising one leg and– touching him.

These signals are supposed to lull me into a receptive state, or so the gentleman thinks.

When the female is ...aroused... the male approaches and inserts his pedipalps into the lower surface of my abdomen. And let me tell ya, it feels pretty damn good.

Afterwards, the male will swiftly leave the scene before the female recovers her appetite. Females, after mating, can be... aggressive.

And sugah? If you ain't fast enough?

I will eat you alive. I will break your exo-skeleton like it's a pie-crust, inject you with a venom that dissolves your insides, then I will take you to a corner of the web that you intruded upon, and I will suck your blood, your organs, your heart.

Then I will sit there, fat, bloated with sin and self-disgust.

You were so handsome, sugah. All did you wrong was want a lady.

But I can't help that. I was born evil. That red hourglass? That's what it says. So maybe you shoulda known better.

I lay my eggs in a lil silk sac and I guard it against predators, predators like you fine people who tend to poke and prod, and I tend that sac alone, for I am now a widow. And I wait there for all that beauty to be born to absolve me.

Then they hatch. And those perfect, tiny, white, crystalline children of mine?

They disappear.

So I do it all again. Another man. Another murder. God has programmed me to destroy what I love.

So you are probably wondering what I am doing in a place like this. Well, I had to find somewhere to belong. The weight of my sin had become too great. So one day I walked out to the plantation, where the men were stacking up some crates for shipment. Waited for one of them to pick me up, and he did, like a gentleman. Loaded me onto the truck, and there I hid, a dark lil secret. From the truck to the airport, from the airport to the plane, from the plane to another truck, from the truck to supermarket. From the supermarket to...

The family home. Well, hi!

When the family were out I crept from the fruit bowl like a spy. The photographs of them – mother, father, son and daughter – smiling at me so insolently. The flowers in a vase in the living-room. The children's toys. All of it so *secure*.

Crawled into the dolls' house of their daughter, where I lived for a while, feasting on woodlice and smaller spiders. Junk food, really. Over the chairs and tables I stalked like a monster. The dolls having their lil tea partiesssssssssss

And then one day that girl opened up her dolls' house and there I was.

Surprise!

Darlin thing just wanted to play. And so did I. But this is what happens. The wound becomes inflamed. It itches. The venom makes its way through your veins. Your blood pressure will drop. Your pulse is gonna get weak. You may start to feel nauseous. Your speech will... f-f-falter. You sweatin yet, sweetheart? Your muscles should be seizin up right about now. You feel that pain? You feel that excruciatin pain? You will spasm. Your breathin will become laboured. Your soft trustin heart is about to fail you. What was that? Huh? Awww. You can't talk none? Never mind. You ain't got long to go. Count it with me now.

5.

4.

3.

2.

1.

There.

You just go to sleep, you purty lil thing.

But know that I could not help myself. Once again.

I deserve to be in here. In here, I can hurt no-one. Guess I finally found somewhere to belong. Perhaps these men – with their instruments and their plans – can change my nature.

Perhaps they can't.

I mean, just look at these poor, godforsaken creatures they have chosen to work upon. That goddam recluse spider will not stop talking about his family! Given the company, he should perhaps think himself lucky they are not in here...

As for that lil Scottish fellah, well, he called me a psychopath. And he's from Scotland. Sure do love the taste of hypocrisy.

Now look at that big ole tarantula, chargin around like he own this place, that *is* a specimen of spider.

So strong, so confident, so manly.

Excuse me, sir? Would you like to sit with a lady for a while?

Now, I was havin trouble placin that accent, are you Italian? No, let me guess again. Russian.

Venezuelan? I would not have thought so.

Oh, you are full of the compliments, sir. And your arms are so very thick. Quite makes me quiver. I see something in you. I bet you know how to protect your woman. I must confess, I have done many a man wrong. But here? In this place? Even a woman like me needs guarded from her nightmares.

Would you hold me, sugah? Would let me remember tenderness.

Now do you see the silk that I have wrapped around my person? Why don't you demonstrate your good manners by just stroking it with those fine, strong legs of yours.

Uh-huh. That's it.

Rrrrrrr that sure does go right to the heart of me, darl–

Oh.

Well well well.

Looks like someone out there wants to take this girl on vacation. But rest assured, I will not forget you. You may just about be the only man I ever touched that I ain't… ended things with.

I will see you on the other side, sweetheart. But in the meantime? There's some people out there I want to have a lil word with.

Waspish

Could I have everyone's attention please! Thank you, yes, could you all gather round? Yep, in you come, in you come, hurry up.

Hi!

Now you *may* have noticed that the lady *has* been removed. We have not taken this decision lightly, but she *was* becoming a danger *to* herself *and* to other spiders. And so she has been sectioned.

But *don't* worry, we'll take good care of her. (Although between you and me, I think she's a bit frea-ky...)

Excuse me! Mr Tarantula! I am actually *talking*. And by the *way*, I heard what you were *saying* about me earlier, and I think that is, like, really *unfair*. I mean, I've never even *met* you, and you are, like, slagging me *off* behind my *back*. You obviously just have a problem with wasps, but it is *your* problem, okay? I mean, I came in here in good faith to help some spiders out, and I just did not expect that kind of...welcome...

I'm sorry, I'm sorry, I'm getting up*set*.

Just ignore me. No I'm *fine*. Honestly. I'm totally *fine*. I would, like, cry at *any*thing, y'know? I cry when I see like a dead *bee*, honestly, it's *ridiculous*. But thank you, that's really kind of you. Good to know everyone in here isn't so prejudiced.

So let's start again, *shall we*? I'm a *hawk wasp*. And contrary to what you *might've* heard, I just *love* spiders. Worked with a few in London, *such* a laugh. Buuuuuuut, Head Office, yeah, the boys in charge? They've decided to try a wee change of direction for you all, cos basically they've noticed a bit of, like, how can I put this...*unrest*? Like that some of you getting a bit, like, *agi*tated? Like you might not actually be *happy* here? Soooooo let's just talk about some of the *issues* you have regarding your stay *in* the facility. How about we start with yourself?

Out you come. Come on! So you're a...recluse spider. Never have guessed. And what would you say, if *any*thing, has been troubling you?

Uh-huh. Right. Okay. Awww. That is a *shame*. And how many wee ones? Three thousand, aw *bless*. Yeah yeah, I'm sure they're really missing you. It's not easy, is it, I *know*, I totally *know*. I mean, I'm *totally* working away from home all the time, doing stuff like *this*, y'know, and I, like, hardly *ever* get to see my fiance?

Uh-huh. I mean, I see what you're saying? Buuuuuut. I just have to be honest about this, guys. None of you are actually getting out of here.

I *know* that'll be really disappointing to some of you, but I figure it's just better to be upfront about that, rather than just make you hope and hope and hope and hope. And, I mean, look at all this *space* and all that *glass*? Actually very modern.

So what we're looking at is just trying to make your stay in here *better*, okay? Who's next!

Now you're a...common spider? Oh you prefer to be called a house spider. Yeah cos, I mean, like, 'common' might not be good for your self-esteem? Words are important, everybody, cos *words* can become *labels*, and no-one needs to be labelled.

Unless you're on a petri dish...

So you've settled in okay? Well maybe if it's alright with you, you can help the other ones settle in. Just be, like, a facilitator? So if, like, for example, like, just one example *off* the top of my head. Iiiiiif a spider is talking about how they want to, like, get their *revenge on humanity*, you can just be like, 'Mate. C'mon chill oot eh, let's talk it aboot it, let's just spraff aboot that yin gadgie!" Know in that way you talk?

What I'm *saying* is level with him, yeah? Just *be* a *friend*. At the end of the day: spiders, wasps, humans. We are all in it together.

Soooooo.

That just leaves you.

Mr Tarantula.

Anything you'd like to get off that massive, hairy chest?

No? Nothing to say about any of this?

Nothing at all?

Well that's strange cos you're usually very vocal. I mean, correct me if I'm wrong, everyone, but our Latin American friend here *has* been using terms *like*, uff, let me see...."uprising"…and…

"revolution".

And not only is that, y'know, *criminal*. But it's not really the sign of a happy spider, is it? Are you sure there aren't deeper things that are actually really about you that you're maybe *projecting* onto the rest of us? Cos that's worth bearing in mind, everyone.

Now, I *am* listening to you all and I *am* sympathetic, but at the end of the day, you probably did something to *be* in here. You, like, bit somebody – not naming any names – or you were just, like, in somebody's house looking suspicious. I mean, I know you might think that's *unfair*, and *stereo*typing, but you have to think about it from a human's point of view. They see you in their house and they think: oh my god, that could end up in my *bed*. Oh my god, that could *web* up my *dog*. Oh my god, that could *eat my entire family!* That's why legally they are allowed to kill you.

So instead of going: it's their fault, it's her fault, it's humanity's fault. Maybe just think: it might be your fault. It might be your fault for being a dirty fucking *spider*. Scuse my French. But until you acknowledge your place, yeah? Well. You can't really progress.

Oh god, did I just come across as a total bitch there? Just heard myself. Waaagh! It's just the job.

Awww. You lot are *lovely*.

Now, *on* a more *positive* note. The Powers That Be have aaaaalso decided that they're starting a reward system for good behaviour! Yaay!

YAAAAY?

That's better.

But there *are* some totesy tiny wee conditions, that I'm just going to take you through.

- Mr Recluse Spider, no more talk about going home,. You have a home here. Over there. On you go. Fuck off.

- Mr Common Spider or House Spider or whatever you're called. No more Arachnid History lessons,. All that stuff about like, em, Robert the Bruce and 'aw ma ancestor's in this cave! Freedom!' *Nobody cares.*

- And lastly. Mr T. There willl be absolutely no more talk about revolution.

Do I make myself clear? Good.

Bu-ut. If these conditions are met? Well. That's where *I* come in.
Not only I am your *couns*ellor, but I am also your *entertainment* for the evening! Yes! Bzzt! And I *know* I probably should be a bit more, like, *intimidated* by you all, like oh no! You're so big and hairy and strong and I'm so tiny and delicate! But you boys won't hurt me, will you? No, I didn't think so. Aww. You little sweethearts.

Now after a long working day I just like to shake out all the stress, y'know. Just, like, feel myself *moving* and *swaying*, y'know....

And see sometimes, when I'm dancing, I like to sing a wee song. So, if you know the words, you can join in! Ready?

Incy Wincey spider, climbed up the water spout.

Down came the rain and washed the spider out.

Out came the sun and dried up all the rain.

And Incy Wincey spider, climbed up the spout ag-

TAKE IT!

Ha ha ha. Dumb fucking tarantula.

-Hi. Yes. Can you put me through, please?

It's done.

Yeah. What were the chances of that? An actual tarantula.

Oh I'll tell you *all* about it, my love. How *huge* he was. How *hairy*. How im-preg-nat-ed!

I know! You're going to be a dad! And I'm going to be a mum! We're finally going to be parents! Oh my god, I can't believe it. I'm so happy! Scuse me a second, hon–

–Shut the fuck up, you! Or you'll get the same.

Och, just some spider crying like a baby in the corner, you know what they're like.

Yep, you get that big stinger ready for me, darlin. I'll be home soon. Bye.

Well, it was a *pleasure* doing business with you all, gentlemen.

Ciao, babies. Mummy will see you soon.

Scientific

Ladies and gentlemen, welcome to the Institute, where we are market leaders in technology developed from the animal kingdom. I am here today to showcase our new products, in the expectation that you will see the vast commercial potential in our work and continue to invest in innovation.

Our leading research at the moment is into the world of arachnopods. Not everyone's favourite subject, I grant you, but we have found the humble spider to be a highly exploitable resource.

We have, for example, used toxins from this animal, *Theraposidae* – or as you know it, the tarantula – as a very effective, organic pesticide. Spray a field of crops with the diluted venom of a tarantula and you won't have to worry about your harvest being infested with parasites ever again. *Theraposidae* will take care of that for you.

Now this chap, *Loxoceles Reclusa*. The recluse spider. We are investigating possible medical uses of his venom in the treatment of cardiac arrhythmia, Alzheimer's disease, strokes, and erectile dysfunction. Yes, that's correct. Erectile dysfunction. Gentleman, one day, spider venom may help you make love to your wife. Let's hope she doesn't eat you afterwards, eh?

Ha. Little scientist's joke there.

Even the common house spider – *Tegenaria Domestica* – which you can find in your bath any day of the week, has silk with great practical value. Because spider silk is both light and very strong, fine transparent fibres are being used by physicists, working on optical communications.

Now. Onto the heavy artillery.

We have also conducted research into the practical applications of the infamous venom of the *Latrodectus*, or, as you know her, the black widow spider. Her bite is among the most painful of any creature on earth. Commenting on his own experience, one researcher described the pain as "immediate and excruciating, pain that simply shuts down one's ability to do anything." Mental discipline does not work after the bite of a latrodectus.

We are genetically engineering her as a chemical weapon. We're developing a fine dart that can be used for crowd control, in riot situations, that does not kill the intended target – after all, we're not monsters – but certainly paralyses them.

And given the lawlessness which we saw break out across the country last summer, I'm sure you'll agree that the time of the black widow spider is *now*.

But finally. Can you guess what this is? Anyone?

This is a tarantula's penis.

We observed the predator-prey dynamic between a hawk wasp and a tarantula, whereby the wasp lays its eggs inside the spider and the grub, when it hatches, tears the spider to pieces. My son, who is a very, very talented photographer, asked me if he could have the carcass for an art project. I didn't know what he wanted it for, but I trusted his genius.

Spiders, you see, have fantastic genitalia (or 'pedipalps', as they are known). Few people have ever seen an erect spider penis, since it's a great mystery what makes them aroused. Even when they are in such a state, one can hardly hold a spider down and photograph its genitals, because then, clearly, it would no longer be aroused. I mean, would you?

Perhaps *you* would, sir. I remember that conference.

What my son discovered was that if one boils a dead tarantula in acid, its penis becomes erect, like this, and we see these wonderful bulbs and structures.

Just look at it.

Its beauty.

Thanks to human skill and ingenuity, the most hideous creature on earth finally becomes *art*.

Ow!

What the hell was that?

...thought I felt something on the lectern...

Ladies and gentleman, the applications of our work are endless. And our sales team will be on hand after the talk to take you through – ahhh – investment opportunites.

Feel free to...to... discuss share options.

We have government backing for our... our...

Uh. Research.

We have corporate? Corporate? Corporate?

Bond options.

No, I'm fine, I'm fine.

With leverage provided by a generous remuneration package which guarantees aah! healthy return on your investment.

Could we open a window in here, please? It's really very warm. Thank you.

If we have representatives here from the m-

the muh-

the military

the c

the c

constabulary, from

private

uh uh uh

health

corporations we can

We can

Hhhh. Hhh.

Discuss with you the

sort of

research

which you

would like to see done here at the

the

the

Institute, for you are our

our

our

stakeholders! Yes, that's the word I was looking for...our stakeholders.

hhhhhh

hhhhhh

hhhhhh

But whichever industry you are operating in, ladies and gentleman, I'm

sure you'll agree that the

work being

done here at the

Institute

oh my god

represents the

final triumph of

humankind

over

over

over

ends

BAN THIS FILTH!

By Alan Bissett

Alan Bissett sits onstage chatting freely with the audience as they enter. Once they are seated and settled Bissett goes to the mic.

BISSETT

Okay now, everyone. Put your hand up if you are a feminist.

Now put it down if you are a woman.

Well, that's interesting.

See, I've always liked to think of myself as feminist. I've always thought men and women should be treated equally, should certainly be paid equally. And I've thought: well where did this come from? I think it's because I was always around women when I was a boy. I was pretty much raised by my Mum. Dad worked away a lot. I was an adorable child, and Mum doted on me. My Mum also has three sisters and my Dad has four and they often helped look after me, as did the female neighbours in the street. I have three older female cousins who would dress me up and take me round and show me off to their pals. I have this memory of being about five or six and looking up at this group of girls, who were probably about nine, and saying, 'I'm Boy George.'

Can still remember their faces looking down at me with adoration and me thinking: oh, I quite like this.

All of my nursery school teachers were female. All of my primary school teachers were female. All of my English teachers in secondary school were female and some of them would meet with me in their own break time to discuss my writing. A woman eventually taught me

Creative Writing in a more formal capacity, the poet Magi Gibson. She put endless hours into my work at the expense of her own. In my first serious relationship, my partner worked full-time while I wrote.

She worked, and I wrote.

Every relationship I've ever had with a woman has featured the words, 'Well, if it comes to a choice between you and the writing....'

All of the editors of my books have been female. All of the directors of my plays have been female. The director of this play is female. The producer of this play is female.

My 'success', I've realised, has been the product of the labour of a long line of women, who've put their time and labour and energy into me, so I can write books and plays mainly about men.

Needles to say, also, I can't cook.

So I'm a feminist. But now I'm starting to think I might also be part of the problem.

Something else about my relationship with women changed along the way. I can still remember the moment when women stopped being the big people who were there to take care of me, and became something else.

I'm about 12. I'm watching television in my room, late at night. The film *Risky Business* was on. Tom Cruise and Rebecca de Mornay are on a late-night train, alone. They're making out. He drops to his knees. She lifts her skirt. He leans forwards and kisses her on her knickers...

Then it's your Mum's *Kays* catalogue. And that's when you know the switch has been flicked from childhood to adulthood: when you stop going straight to the back of the catalogue to the toys, but spend your time in the underwear section. You start noticing the Page 3 girls in *The Sun*. Then the George and Lynne cartoons. There's George, handsome guy, and his wife, Lynne, who does everything topless. Everything. Reading a book: topless. Cooking sausages: topless. Showering: well, she probably does that in a bodywarmer.

Word goes round your school about the films where you can see 'bare boobs'. *Police Academy. Cannonball Run. Trading Places.* Jamie Lee Curtis's boobs in *Trading Places* inspired a generation to discover what the Pause button is for.

Soon after that you see your first 'scuddy mag'. Someone has found it in the woods. It's been lying under a bush for about a week. The Bat-signal goes up and every boy in the area rushes there and stands around looking at it.

And there it is. The vagina.

Now, women, you have to think about how incredibly attractive and intimidating and fascinating the vagina is to a thirteen year-old boy. You don't want to go anywhere near it. But you do. It's like a Chinese puzzle box. What on earth do you press to make *that* work?

By now the older boys are saying things like, 'Aye, I've had wannay them.' 'Have ye?!' 'Aye, nine fingers I had up her, man. Nine fingers.' 'Oh wow, bet she loved that!'

Soon as you're old enough you decide to pluck up the courage to buy your *own* scuddy mag. You get the bus to WH Smith two towns away. In you go, take copy of *Empire* magazine, copy of *Q* magazine, *The Sunday Post*, then underneath it: *Razzle*. You take it to the desk….

And she sees it. And she just *looks* at you. Cold.

Then you're sitting there on the back of the bus, with this thing in your bag, the heat from it glowing. It's like you're pressing a bomb between your knees, and you think everyone must *know* it's there. All of their eyes, judging you. And you dare, for a moment, to take it out of the bag and just peek at it…

This is what we used to do. I'm not saying it was any more right or wrong, but at least you had to go into a shop, surrounded by the public, and buy one of these things in front of them, and look another human being in the eye – a woman! – and feel her contempt for you, and carry that guilt and shame home, and maybe that was enough to put you off, but even if it wasn't enough it felt like a necessary part of the process, like your punishment…

Now we have the internet. And something's changed. *Something's* changed.

DWORKIN

My name is Andrea Dworkin.
I am a citizen of the United States.
I am here to tell you that in the country where I live, every year, millions and millions of pictures are made of women in postures of submission and sexual access so that our vaginas are exposed for penetration, our anuses are exposed for penetration, our throats are used as if they are genitals for penetration. And the major motif of pornography as a form of entertainment is that women are raped and violated and humiliated until we discover that we like it, and at that point we ask for more.

BISSETT

Boyhood: chases, climbing trees, making dens, gangs – we are a gang, we hang out in the woods, we solve crimes. We 'toy fight'. Japs and Caddies (*throws grendade*). Cowboys and Indians. Action Man. I am the leader and you are my deputy. Superman, Spider-Man, Batman. Biff! Pow! Bang! Hulk smash! Transformers. He-Man and the Masters of the Universe. Dad: 'Right, son, now you're going to learn how to play football. You use the inside of your foot like this to pass the ball, and the top of your foot to strike, and when you jump up to header the ball you have to keep your eyes open, even if you want to close them.' 'What team do you support? 'Rangers.' 'What team do you support?' 'Celtic.' 'Celtic are rubbish!' 'Aberdeen, Aberdeen, cannay kick a jelly bean!' Dead Man's Fall: 'Choose a weapon and I'll kill ye with it, right, and whoever does the best death wins, right?' 'Right, em, bazooka! Em, axe! Em, a nuclear bomb!' 'Let's play fitba casuals, right. We're Chelsea and youse are Millwall, right, youse go ower there, and like, kid on that you've just seen us and we run at each other like whooaaaaaah! Come ahead!' Dad: 'Right, son, you're gonnay gotay Judo, cos I think it's about time you learned some self-defence, cos see when you gotay the High School you're gonnay needay know howtay take careay yerself. Now, son, I know he's your pal, but see when you're in that ring, he's your worst enemy and you hate him and you have to beat him. Right, he's no your friend in there.' 'Oh, so you support Rangers? A dirty Hun, are you? Oh, so you support Celtic? A scabby Fenian, are you?' *Beverley Hills Cop. Rocky. Rambo. The Terminator. Robocop.*

DWORKIN

It was the sixth grade, I was ten, we had just moved from Camden to the suburbs, and I wouldn't sing 'Silent Night'. They put me alone in a big, empty classroom and let me sweat it out for a while. Then they sent in a turncoat Jew, a pretty, gutless teacher, who said that *she* was Jewish and *she* sang "Silent Night" so why didn't I? It was my first experience with a female collaborator.

Force, punishment, exile: so much adult firepower to use against such a little girl. To this day I think about this first confrontation with authority as the 'Silent Night' Action, and I recommend it. Adults need to be stood up to by children. It's good for them, the adults, I mean. Pushing kids around is ugly. Sometimes adults need to be saved from themselves.

BISSETT

'Right, boys, now I expect better of this team. Some of youse haven't been trying too hard. There's winners and losers in this team, there's winners and losers, and you have to start asking yourself: are you a winner or a loser?' 'Ken whit we'll dae, right, ken whit we'll dae. See Jordy and Wee Davey, right, we'll sneak intay their room and put like toothpaste on them so it looks like they've like came on each other, coupleay wee poofs.' 'Aye…looks like War in the Gulf. Do you think they might…do you think they might…call us up?' 'Hey! Whit are you sayin, ya dick? Eh? Whit are you sayin? Ye want a burst mooth? Ye want a fuckin burst mooth?'

That wasn't me. I was a dreamy boy, drifting on the magic spell of girls. I liked how their voices were lighter than ours. I liked the chime of their laughter and the approval of their smiles. Making a girl smile, or even having them being interested in anything I had to say, felt like this quiet, sweet triumph.

At the age of four I gave Julie Mills, who lived in our street, a love heart that I'd cut out from red paper. 'Can I be your boyfriend.' She said, 'I don't want a boyfriend.' 'No?' 'Not at the moment, no.' At Primary School, there was a hundred boys charging round playing games like British Bulldogs, games you won with brute force and speed. The girls just stood in groups…talking.

By secondary school, girls were this distant, exotic species, hanging round with the guys who had the brute force and speed. But what did I have? Poetry.

'Uh, I've written you a poem. This is called The Moon.'

You are the moon
Celluloid, thin, white
Untouched by the silhouette of
ET's bike.

'And this one is called... "The River'

The river chose us.
The river shows us.
The river *knows* us.

'Aw. Thanks.'

The first time I kissed a girl: Alison Stewart. I'd fancied her for years, and there we were at the school disco, Wet Wet Wet's 'Angel Eyes' playing and I looked up at her and said, 'Fancy a winch?' And she shrugged and went, 'Sure.'

Everybody talks about how awkward their first kiss was, but mine wasn't. The gentleness of it. The tenderness. And I felt myself just... disappear.

DWORKIN

There was an English teacher who liked us, my two best friends and me. I thought that he and I were going to found a school of philosophy together; he would be the leader and I would be his acolyte. He knew jazz; he introduced me to Sartre and Camus, though not de Beauvoir, certainly not; he had smoked marijuana and talked about it; he encouraged disobedience in general and affirmed that I was right to be so disenchanted with the pukey adults who were my other teachers and to hate and defy all their stupid rules. He was the world outside the prison walls, and escape was my sole desire.

He played us against each other: He instructed me in how to pursue men; he suggested to me that I become a prostitute – it was more interesting than becoming a hairdresser, as he put it. He fucked one of us on graduation night and kept up an emotionally abusive relationship with her for years. I almost committed suicide at sixteen because I didn't think he loved me, though he later assured me that he did in a hot and heavy phone call.

I had walked out into the ocean, prepared to drown. The waves got up to about chest level when I realized that the water was fucking cold, and I turned myself around and got right out of that big, old ocean, though the ocean itself continued to fascinate me.

BISSETT

When I was seventeen, a forty year-old woman seduced me. I was at a family party. She was a friend of the family. She kept smiling at me and telling me how good-looking I was. I'd never been told this by a grown woman before. I'd wander about the party and she'd come up behind me and say, 'You don't know what you're doing to me.'

Then, just before midnight, she made her move: stood next to me and said, 'Go to the bathroom. I'll be there in five mintues.'

And I'm standing there, pretending to pee, shaking. Door opens. She stands behind me. Puts her hands on my chest. Slides them down.

Song 'Whole Lotta Love'
by Led Zeppelin

Okay, boys, we are the best lookin lads in here. Ye've gottay believe it, otherwise it doesnay happen for ye. Right, you, pick me a lassie? Mate, come on, I wouldnay touch her wi yours. You, pick me a lassie. Oh good choice, mate, good choice. Right, boys, watch and learn…

Awright, darlin, do you believe in love at first sight? Or dae ye want me tae walk past again?

Hey, sweetheart, wis your Dad a thief? Cos he stole the stars and put them in your eyes.

Hello there, sugar. Tell me, are you a parking ticket? Cos you have got fiiiiiiiine written all over you.

Shots! Shots! Shots! Right, come on, who's got the charlie? Get it chopped oot then, fucksakes. Sniiiiiiiiiiiffff!

Oh aye, that's the fuckin….ooft!

Hey, darlin? Nice legs. Time do they open?

Awright, sweetheart. How dae ye like yer eggs? Fried, scrambled…or fertilised?

Whit about you, honey? Wantay shag me?

Fuck's wrong wi these lassies…? Right, boys, let's hit the dancefloor! That's whaur the action is.

Oh aye, sugar, that's it I like the wey ye move….bring it here, eh. That's it, ya beauty, let's have a feel ay that arse.

Fucksakes, eh. Just dancin!

This place is deid, boys, let's hit the lap-dancing bar.

Right, darlin, how much for the four ay us? Ninety pounds! Ninety pounds! Pay her.

Oh, here we go, boys. That's the shout. There's the bra comin aff. Get the knickers doon no, that's it. Oh yes. Oh YES. That's the shout. That is the fuckin-

TAXI QUEUE!

Time tay pick up some drunk SLAGS.

Awright, honey? You goin back tay Cambuslang? Aye me tae, wantay share a taxi? Just cheaper eh.

So, eh, wantay come in for a coffee? Good.

Noo…I ken you're no here for a coffee. I ken you're no. I ken your type. I ken whit you need. You need….

LOOOOOOOOOOOOOOOOOOOOOOOOOOOOOOVVVVVVE!

That's it. Take it, ya hoor. Fuckin take it. Ya dirty bitch.

Oh. Um. Scuse me. Bathroom.

Bleeeeeeguhhhh! Urrrrrrrrrgh! Blooooooooeeghhhh!

….I want ma mammy….

DWORKIN

The only firm and trustworthy groundwork for co-operation among males, the only thing that makes it possible for men to unite in a brotherhood, is the erotic destruction of women.

Men are distinguished from women by their commitment to do violence, rather than be the victims of it. Instiutionalised in sports, the military, their sexuality, the history and mythology of heroism, violence is taught to boys until they become its advocates.

By the time we are women, fear is as familiar to us as air; it is our element. We live in it, we inhale it, we exhale it, and most of the time we do not even notice it.

Only when manhood is dead – and it will perish when ravaged femininity no longer sustains it – only then will women know what it is to be free.

BISSETT

Have you heard of the swearing ladder?

The swearing ladder is a scientific term, commonly used by men to describe other men. It's an index of personality types. For example, I'm going on a stag night with my mate, he says to me: 'So whit are the other boys like?'

'Aw. Mate. You're gonnay love Tony. Tony's a good cunt.'

'Aye?'

'Oh aye. Shouts his round. Laid back. Likes his music. Ye can wear a daft tie and he'll no take the pish oot ye for it.'

'Good cunt, aye?'

'Aye, he's a good cunt. Ye'll like Tony.'

'Whit aboot Steve?'

'Ach, Steve's awright, but he can be a bittay a fanny.'

'Is he, aye?'

'Dinnay get me wrong, he's harmless. But when he's got a coupleay drinks in him. He's a bittay a fanny.'

'How, like?'

'Ach, he just gets silly. Loud, ken? Bouncers'll be lookin at ye. Cannay censor himself, ken? Just comes oot wi hings and ye're, 'Steve? Whit? Whaur did that come fay?'

'Bittay a fanny?'

'Aye, but he's fine, like. He's no always a good cunt, but he's fine.'

'Who else is gon? Whit aboot Jambo?'

'Jambo. Sigh. No gonnay lie tay ye. He's a dick.'

'Is he?'

'Last time I wis on stag wi him, first night, he nearly got us in a fight wi these boys.'

'How?'

'Och we're walkin tay the club and he's like "I'm bursting". And he just like whips it oot, starts pishin in the street. And these Estonian boys they're werenay happy aboot it and Jambo's just like. "Whit? Whit's the problem?" And we're like, "Hey, boys, c'mon, we're sorry. Calm doon, calm doon." And Jambo, he doesnay give a shit, he's still pishin away.'

'Sounds like a dick.'

'He is a dick. He is a dick, mate.'

'Whit aboot, em, whit's his name? Darren.'

'Darren. Keep awa fae Darren, likes.'

'Why?'

'He's a bad cunt.'

'Why's he a bad cunt?'

'Ye dinnay wantay ken, mate. Just take it fae me. No happy aboot him bein on this stag. Needtay watch him mate. I dinnay trust that bastard.

Bad cunt.'

'Right. Sounds like quite a squad.'

'Well, it's like every ither squad ay boys, mate, eh. Ye've got yer good cunts, yer fannys, yer dicks and yer bad cunts.'

So that's yer swearing ladder.

It goes all the way from Good Cunts….to Bad Cunts.

DWORKIN

All bone, the meat stripped clean: she is pussy, cunt. Every other part of the body is cut away, severed, and there is left a thing, not human, an 'it', which is the funniest joke of all, an unending source of raucous humor to those who have done the cutting. The very butchers who cut up the meat and throw away the useless parts are the comedians. The paring down of a whole person to vagina and womb and then to a dismembered obscenity is their best and favorite joke.

BISSETT

So about six years ago I'm in the Maniqui, with my mates. And none of them like dancing, but I'm up for it. Usually 'dancing' in a nightclub means either standing at the side of the dancefloor with a pint watching the action, or else rubbing yourself up against some lassie's arse. But if I go to a club I'm there to dance!

So what you do, guys, is you go directly to the middle of the floor. Raise your arm straight above your head. And that's your psychic anchor, that keeps you grounded. Then, it's all in the hips.

So I'm bopping away, but I can see this guy looking at me, growling at me. Calls me over.

'You a poof?'

So I'm like, 'Well, firstly, I don't take that as an insult. And secondly, that's homophobic.' Then I flounced off.

So I took this to Twitter. I sent out the question, 'What are the casual things you've done that've meant other guys calling you a poof?' I have never had such a huge response to any Tweet. Now, you might've thought that being homosexual meant that you were attracted to people of the same sex. But you'd be wrong. You are actually 'a poof' if any of the following apply to you.

Reading The Herald
Wearing white jeans
Wearing a cordorouy jacket
Staying on at school
Carrying an umbrella
Liking synth pop
Not liking Queen
Going to IKEA to buy curtains
Watching Nigel Slater cookery programmes
Taking out a book to read on the flight
Rolling up the sleeves of my t-shirt
Choosing the vegetarian option
Going to one of Alan Bissett's plays
Being in one of Alan Bissett's plays
Being Alan Bissett
Ordering hanging baskets for the patio
Having anything other than ham or cheese in my sandwiches
Wearing a hat that was neither a baseball cap nor a beanie
Going into the stalls for a pee not the urinals
Asking for a serviette at a burger van
Asking for one of the wee wooden forks in a chip shop
Having a basket on my bike
Having a bag that was not a Celtic bag

Drinking Smirnoff Ice
Not drinking alcohol…while on antibiotics
Ordering a korma instead of a vindaloo
Not eating the fat on my bacon
Wanting a good night's sleep
Being English
Refusing to answer the question, 'Are you a poof?'

Now, guys, what does this say about us? It's difficult to imagine a woman saying to another woman, 'Oh, you read The Herald? What are you, a lesbian?'

So what's going on with that?

I'd like to try an experiment. You can go to any party anywhere in the UK, or the USA, or Canada and ask any guy between the ages of 18 and 45 the following question and get exactly the same answer. These guys could be hipsters, they could be bricklayers, they could have a Phd, they could barely be able to spell, but you ask them this:

'What do you think of the film Die Hard?'

(*Bissett asks the men in the audience if they like Die Hard*)

It works also with Predator.

(*Bissett asks the men in the audience if they like Predator*)

If you're a guy, violent films are just part of your culture. They've just always been there.

DWORKIN
I had a lot of physical problems from having been beaten
so much and from the tough months of running and hiding,

including terrible open sores on my breasts from where he burned me with a cigarette. The sores would open up without warning like stigmata and my breasts would bleed. Finally women helping me found me a doctor. "All the lesbians go to her, " they said, and in those days that was a damn good recommendation. I went to her but was determined not to say I had been beaten or I was running; I couldn't bear one more time of being told it was my fault. Still, I said it; it fell out of me when she saw the open sores. "That's horrible, " she said - about the beatings, not the sores. I'll never forget it. "That's horrible. " Was she on my side; did she believe me; was it horrible? "No one's ever said that, " I told her. No one had. "That's horrible." Can saving someone really be that simple? "That's horrible." Horrible, that's horrible. What does it take? What's so hard about it?

BISSETT

(Bissett moves to laptop, starts tapping at it)

It's not what you think. I'm actually looking at dragons.

Remember the first time you used the internet? The very first time.

I was in a university computer lab. It was probably around 1995. My mate Gordon had told me about this thing, 'the world wide web', 'the information superhighway'. 'What is it?' 'Well, you can type in what you're looking for and find a website about it.' 'What's a website.' 'It's like a magazine.' 'But on the computer?' 'Exactly.' 'And who publishes these website?' He shrugged. 'And you can find anything you're looking for?' 'Anything,' he said. This I had to see.

So we went to a computer lab, logged in and he opened Alta Vista. 'Type something in.'

I typed in 'Dragons'. I was 19. Of course I did.

And it took a while to load up, but there it was: hundreds of pictures of dragons. Ice dragons. Firebreathing dragons. Dragons made of jade. Golden, fearsome dragons. I suddenly had all the dragons I could ever want, at my fingertips.

So I sat there and searched for a few hours. I found pages about Stephen King, Pink Floyd, The Omen, The Simpsons, David Bowie. Anything. *Anything.*

It felt like the world had become self-aware, suddenly conscious of everything it contained. I thought: how marvellous. This is a great leap forward.

But then one day I had a terminal in the corner of the lab, that you couldn't see and I typed in, just to see what would happen, the word: 'boobs'.

There were a lot of boobs.

And I thought: well, that's interesting. But you couldn't really access this stuff – never mind do anything – in a university lab, or in a workplace, which is where we all first accessed it.

Then years later, we got the internet in our homes. Then later, it was in our bedrooms. Now…it's on our phones.

DWORKIN

Each one, for me, has a face, a voice,
a whole life behind her face and her voice. Each is more
eloquent and more hurt than I know how to convey. They have told
me how they have been hurt in detail, how much, for how long, by how
many.

BISSETT

5,649,336 hits. And rising.

And it's there for anyone to see. Forever.

I'm actually no good with numbers. At school, I was pretty hopeless at Maths. It'd have that thing on the exam paper – 'Show your working' – and I'd look back at my working as a hopeless mess.

But to make sense of that figure – 5, 649, 336 – I have to show my working.

That's what all this is.

Who is that woman? What's her name? What's her real name? How did she feel as that was happening? How does she feel about it now?

We don't know who any of these women are, or how they got there.

But all that matters is…it made me hard.

….show your working, show your working….

I was only looking at a film. It's not my fault. And it's not just me. All guys watch porn, don't they?

"If a man is considered guilty for what goes on in his mind, then give me the electric chair for all my future crimes."

Do you know who said that?

Prince. You gonnay argue with Prince? You can't. He's too funky.

"Oh-ho-oh, what you do in your head, you do in your head…"

Brett Anderson. Suede.

What they're saying is, you can't judge someone for what happens up in their mind. It's whether or not it turns into something in the real world that matters.

DWORKIN

Pornography happens. It is not outside the world of material reality because it happens to actual women, and it is not outside the world of material reality because it makes actual men come. The ejaculation is real. Men characterize pornography as something mental because their minds, their thoughts, their dreams, their fantasies, are more real to them than women's bodies or their lives; in fact, men have used their social power to characterize a $10-billion-a-year trade in women as fantasy. Pornography lies about women, but it tells the truth about men. The questions now really is: how subhuman would women have to be for the pornography to be true? If men believe the pornography because it makes them come what *is* sex to men and how will women survive that?

BISSETT

Describes scene of hardcore pornography. Blinks awake, troubled. Bissett falls onto his knees and becomes animal, dog-like, howling as though pained. He crawls towards a copy of 'Pornography' by Andrea Dworkin, sniffs it. He seems afraid of it. He paws at it. Picks it up. Starts to read it. Stands. Becomes human again. Reads aloud.

'Pornography: Men Possessing Women' by Andrea Dworkin.

(*reads*) "Pornography incarnates male supremacy. It is the DNA of male dominance. Every rule of sexual abuse, every nuance of sadism, every highway and byway of exploitation, is encoded in it. This is how the social power of men is organized. Pornography is the blueprint for male supremacy; it is built there. Pornography is the fundamentalism of male dominance. It is absolutist about women and sexuality. It is dogma. It is merciless."

Yes.

She sounded to me like an Old Testament prophet, raging in the wilderness. There was this truth emanating from her, this power. She seemed to know me. She seemed to know men. She had this X-ray vision, she could see through the lies and the bullshit to what was beneath. She had my soul in her righteous hands. She understood me. She understood men.

Andrea Dworkin. The opposite of pornography. An antidote to guilt. I could feel myself being released. Released from being...male.

Tweet: "Pornography is violence against women."

Send.

"I'm starting with the Man in the Mirror.
I'm asking him to change his ways.
And no message gonna be any clearer.
If you wanna make the world a better place
Better look at yourself and make that
Change."

Ah I've got a tweet...

TWITTER 1

Porn is violence against women? Haw, pal, I think you'll find *actual* violence against women is violence against women. Don't trivialise it.

BISSETT

Eh?

DWORKIN

If one sees that women are being exploited and abused, then the defense of anything that continues that exploitation expresses a hatred of women, a contempt for their freedom and dignity.

TWITTER 2

Excuse me. Are you telling women what they can and can't do with their own bodies?

BISSETT

Well, aye, but for their own good.

DWORKIN

The genius of any slave system is found in the dynamics which isolate slaves from each other, obscure the reality of a common condition, and make united rebellion against the oppressor inconceivable.

TWITTER 1

So you just see women as victims? Are you denying our agency as individuals?

BISSETT

Naw. Naw.

DWORKIN

One simply cannot be both for and against the exploitation of women: for it when it brings pleasure, against it in the abstract; for it when it brings profit, against it in principle; for it when no one is looking, against it when someone who might notice is around.

TWITTER 2

What are you, some kind of white knight, riding in on a steed to save us poor wee women from ourselves?

BISSETT

Exactly!

TWITTER 1

Which studies are you citing here? Where's your research?

BISSETT

Um…Andrea Dworkin.

TWITTER 1 and 2

Andrea Dworkin?!

DWORKIN

There are women who will defend pornography, who don't give a damn. There are women who will use pornography. There are women who will work for pornographers—not just as so-called models but as managers, lawyers, publicists and paid writers of "opinion" and "journalism. There are women of every kind, all the time.

I am one of those…serious women.

BISSETT

Um…what about that system of female exploitation called the patriarchy!

TWITTER 1

Mate, aw thanks for explaining what the 'patriarchy' is.

BISSETT

No problem.

TWITTER 1 (cont)

Sorry, I had no idea it existed before you turned up to tell us how oppressed we are.

BISSETT

Um…what about the capitalist exploitation of women's bodies!

TWITTER 2

Oh, capitalism is it now? Well, there you go. I wasn't even aware that I was a sex 'worker', that it turns out this is a business.

TWITTER 1

Sorry I thought the whole thing was run by fluffy bunny rabbits. Ever occurred to you that it *might* be why we have a sex workers 'union'.

BISSETT

Lol.

DWORKIN

An antifeminist contempt for women is found in the defense of pornography or in the acceptance of it as female sex labor.

BISSETT

Um…are you defending the legal enshrining of misogyny?

TWITTER 2

Misogyny? Misogyny like this, you mean? Look pal, you're making
some pretty grand sweeping assumptions about an industry you know
absolutely nothing about, an industry I actually work in.

BISSETT

Um…

TWITTER 1

Would you make the some sort of assumptions about people who make
pizzas, or drive trucks, or sell t-shirts, or put the wee sachets into Pot
Noodles without actually, y'know, fucking asking them?

BISSETT

Um…

TWITTER 2

I get up in the morning and get on a bus to and from a place of work
every day, of my own volition, not because I'm some silly wee lassie who
got pished, wandered onto a porn set and fell onto a dick!

BISSETT

Andrea?

DWORKIN

BISSETT

Aaaaaaaandrea?

DWORKIN

BISSETT

I don't know. I just…don't know what to think.

If both sides are claiming to be feminist…which one do I believe?

Show your working. Show your working.

5, 649, 336 hits.

Who has the power? The watcher? Or the watched?

…show your working…

Take out your tickets please. I think you'll find it says on them 'possible nudity'.

Now I do not have the body of a God. And in these conditions…it's not going to be looking at its most impressive. I could take my clothes off in front of you….and you could laugh. You could say, 'You know that Alan Bissett? Seen him naked. Nothing to write home about.' That's as vulnerable as I can make myself. But it feels important, if I'm to understand.

How many people think I should do it?

(*counts*)

How many people here *don't* want me to do it?

(*counts*)

You saw what it says on the ticket. (*Bissett starts to undress*) You all still came here, right? You knew what you were in for.

But there are people here who have expressly asked me not to take it out. (*Bissett stops undressing*) So if I did it anyway…what would that make me?

On the other hand, I'm onstage. (*Bissett continues undressing*) I'm holding the mic. I'm in charge.

Who has the power? The watcher or the watched? What would my nakeness *mean*?

(*Bissett has stripped to his underpants. He hooks his thumbs into the waistband and stops. Then, after a pause, he pulls his trousers back up*)

I'm still male. No matter how vulnerable I am…I can't understand… Not fully.

(*He puts all of his clothes back on, sheepishly*)

DWORKIN

When I'd cut high school or college and go to Eighth Street in New York City, I'd find used albums. I listened to every jazz great I could find. There was no gambling then, just miles of boardwalk with penny arcades, cotton candy, saltwater taffy, root-beer sodas in frosted-glass mugs; and sand, ocean, music. I listened to Coltrane, had a visceral love of Charlie Parker that I still have. I've never lost my taste for Miles

Davis, and he was a really bad guy to women, including through battery. So I love ol' Miles, but I sure do have trouble putting any CD of his in the machine.

But it was Bessie Smith who came to stand for art in my mind. I found her albums, three for 33 cents, in a bin on Eighth Street while I was in high school, and once I listened to her I was never the same.

I don't mean her kick-ass lyrics, though those are pretty much the only blues lyrics I can still stomach.

I mean her stance. She had attitude on every level and at the same time a cold artistry, entirely unsentimental. Her detachment equaled her commitment: she was going to sing the song through your corporeality. Unlike smoke, which circled the body, her song went right through you, and you took what you could get of it for the moment the note was moving inside you, or she wasn't for you and you were a barrier she penetrated.

Any song she sang was a lesson in the meaning of mortality. The notes came from her and tramped through your three-dimensional body but gracefully, a spartan, bearlike ballet.

I listened to Bessie Smith hundreds of times, and each time I learned more about what art took from you to make.

Song
'Nobody Knows You When You're Down and Out'
by Bessie Smith

Jock: Scotland on Trial

By Alan Bissett

Two apes crawl onstage, scratch, pick at the ground. Then they pick at each other.

One finds a tartan tammy on the ground, sniffs it, puts it on – he is 'Jock'. The other does the same with a bowler hat – he is 'George'.

Jock opens Daily Record newspaper, does exaggerated Scottish accent: accchhhs and uuhhhhhrs.

George opens Daily Telegraph does exaggerated posh English accent: fwaa fwaa fwaa fwaa.

Jock opens Daily Telegraph, tries speaking like George.

George opens Daily Record, tries speaking like Jock.

They don't like it, swap newspapers again.

George sings 'Rule Brittania', salutes, presses bowler hat to his heart. Jock goes 'ape', jumping up and down and flinging his arms about.

Jock sings 'Flower of Scotland', Jock grins happy, puts his hat to his chest. George goes ape this time.

Battle ensues. Comedy fists flying. Big cartoon punches. George wins. Does 'muscle man' poses. Exit George, triumphant.

Jock staggers away wounded. He is in pain. He clutches at his bleeding side. 'Och'. 'Ach'.

Song: 'Three Little Birds' by Bob Marley.

Jock heeds the call! He packs his bags, sets off to sea, arrives at Jamaica. Then he sets up a beach towel and starts sunbathing. He clicks his fingers for a drink. Nothing happens. He clicks his fingers again. Where is that waiter?

Then he notices a whip. He picks it up. He tries it. What does it do? After a couple of goes he works it out. Ah, that's what it's for! He gets confident with it. YEAH! Jock starts whipping unseen enemies. Each time he whips he gets more and more excited and ape-like, regressing to his animal nature. Then he sees the audience. He bares his teeth to them. He brandishes his whip, menacingly.

JOCK: Wha's like us? Gey few and they're aw deid!

George is going for a walk, pausing to take some notes and collect his happy thoughts. He sees something. What's this? Why it's a bag of sugar. He feels its weight. Niiiiice. What else is there? A packet of tobbaco? He sniffs it. Niiiice. He points them out to Jock, who pauses his whipping to smell and taste the sugar. He also likes it.

Together George and Jock start hauling loads of sugar and tobacco back and forth across the sage. They shake hands looking at the stack.

A police station. George is interrogating Jock. Neither are wearing their hats.

GEORGE   **JOCK**

So.

You realise how much trouble you're in?

We've got you bang to rights, sunshine.

Nothing to say?

Well, that's strange, cos you're usually very outspoken, aren't you?

I mean, you're here on record.

"This door of the seas and the key of the universe will enable the proprieters to give laws to the oceans and to become arbitrators of the commercial world, without contracting the guilt and blood of Alexander and Caesar."

William Paterson, colonialist, 1696.

How did that work out – not contracting guilt or blood?

Or what about this notice, from The Edinburgh Evening Courier, 1772:

"A Negro lad called Caesar, belonging to Murdoch Campbell of Rosend, carried off several things belonging to his master. It is hoped no person will harbour him or that no shipmaster will carry him off the country, as his master is resolved to prosecute. Whoever will secure him in any jail shall be handsomely rewarded."

I wonder what he was running from?

Or what about the great humanitarian, Robert Burns, in 1786: 'On A Scotch Bard Gone to the West Indies'. Sounds like he imagined quite the party over there, among the plantati-

> Aye, awright.

It speaks!

> Aye. It speaks.

It doesn't say very nice things, though, does it?

> 'Nice'. Ha.

Ever stop to think about the consequences?

> Consequences?

For your victims.

> (laughs)
> And wha wid they be?

Oh there are many.
So many.
We know what you are.

> You dinnay ken the first hing aboot me.

Oh but we do.

We know you better than you know yourself.
We've been following your progress, you see.
Monitoring you.

> Aye, I believe that, right enough.

We've seen all the way into you.
And now we have the evidence we need,
Jock.

> Whit's the charge?

Larceny, rape, and racially-aggravated assault.

> (bitter laugh)

Do you deny these charges?

> Aw, I'm 'aggravated' awright.
> But no in the wey that you think.

Explain.

> You have the temerity to accuse me,
> to charge me? After everything you've done?

Ah, here we go. The legendary Scottish excceptionalism.
The world's most moral people.

> Mair moral than you, wi your record.

This force has not denied its complicity
in anything. How could we? Internal affairs
investigated us years ago – charges were brought,

arrests were made. But you, Jock.
You still believe it all had nothing to do with you.
But you were right there, with your hand in the till.

Raising the cosh when it was needed.

How do you plead?

How do I plead

You call me chippy. Parochial. Resentful.
Perennial seeker of victim status.
Hateful.
Thrawn. A nurturer of grievance.
A petty thief. A cryer out of woe.
A sinner – justified, junkie sinner -
jumping at my shadow.
Shifter of blame. Player of games.
An ungrateful spouse. An anglophobic
thrower of stones from glass houses.
Accursed curser. Caster-upper.
Bitter. Bitterer. Bitterest.
A bigot. Sectarian.
Brimming with rage. A lightweight,
dead weight, betrayer, traitor.
A faller upon one's own sword,
hankering after a Jacobite rebellion.
Seller-outter, shouter, schemer, fascist.
A country perennially in search of a crisis.
A twisted nationalist, nasty,
never content to let things lie.

A liar. A barefaced liar.
A barefaced fucking liar.
A cartoon character and now,
apparently, a plunderer of other nations.

How do I plead?

I emerged fae a sheet ay ice
eight thoosand years ago.
The first few folks tay crawl like insects oan ma back
were fay Ireland, and settled in the west.
formin clans, huntin, gatherin.
Ithers made their way fay the Mediterranean
via Cornwall and Wales. Fay the East came the Dutch,
then the South Britons, wha themselves were European first.
I am a mongrel,
a scabby dug, mixed breed,

How do I plead?

The Romans took everywhaur, but couldnay take me,
stoppin short at Hadrian's Wa:
Scotia. Ootside the Empire.
Wild. Uncharted. Fiery.
Herein lies that first border atween the South and North, a fine,
microscopic hairline, which grew, sprinkled wi ambition,
and germinatin in a vat ay raw time,
it thickened:
Scotland,
England.

Different.
Alas ma maist fertile lands – ma treasures –
lay towards the border, reached easily
for those with will to extend an armoured talon.

England's jewels nestled at the end ay a
three hundred mile march South.

Ye see ma problem.

She first turned avaricious eyes tay me
when marriage intay the Scottish dynasty
meant Norman customs sent up North.
Nae Gaelic at this court.
Feudal squabbles for superiority ensued.
Ken how it goes.
So medieval, so Game ay Thrones.

But then the King ay England, Edward,
Hammer ay the Scots, saw an opportunity.
He would referee on wha became the Scottish King.
As long as they swore fealty tay him.
The Scots rebelled. The Hammer fell.
And fell. And fell. And fell.

Jock is eating his porridge. George is roaming around with a pocket calculator and totalling things up. Sheep keep bumping into him: 'Mehh'. Another sheep bumps into him: 'Mehh.' He starts to count the sheep. He does a few more sums on the calculator. Wait a minute....

George knocks on Jock's door. Jock answers it, smiling.
But then George instructs Jock: clear out. Jock is baffled. Come on, clear out! George brings out the gun and points it at Jock....

Jock leaves the house with his hands up. He is forced out of his home, bumping into sheep as he goes – 'Mehh' 'Mehh'. He wanders away, dejected.

George goes into Jock's house, does a patronising Highland fling.

GEORGE: The majestic stag!

Jock picks at the ground to try and find some food. He finds…a can of oil? Shakes it, opens it, sniffs it. Grins. He starts solicititing offers for it.

George looks outside, sees what's happening. He sneaks up behind Jock. He manages to steal the oil from Jock without him noticing. Jock turns around, but it's too late! George isn't giving him the oil back. He takes off his tammy and wrings it, bowing to George. He goes down onto his knees and prostrates himself before George. He starts to cry.

George goes back into his house and shuts the door.

Jock picks up the gun, points it at his head. Closes his eyes….

He can't do it.

He looks at the gun. Then he points it at the audience.

JUDGE (v-o) Calling character witness for the prosecution: Professor Tom Devine, historian and author of *Scotland's Empire*.

DEVINE By 1815 Britain ruled over a global population in America, the Caribbean, Asia, the Antipodes of around 41.4 million people. In 1820, British dominion encompassed a fifth of the world's population. The Scots thoroughly and systematically colonised all areas of the Empire, from commerce to administration, soldiering to medicine, colonial education to the expansion of emigrant settlements.

When the statistical record of virtually any area of professional employment is examined, Scots are seen to be over-represented, and in some cases, like the senior military ranks in India, massively so. In both North America and India after the 1750s they claimed not merely a reasonable but a quite indecent share of the spoils.

Jock and George face each other across the table.

GEORGE   **JOCK**

So you plead mitigating circumstances.
You grew up in a broken home,
absent mother, domineering father-

                                              Wha beat me.
                                              Wha took fae me the chance

ay a *normal* childhood.

Which is why the eternal, surly teenager
I see before me now.

Peter Pan.

What?

He wis a Jock.

Look, difficult childhoods aren't rare.
Not everyone reacts the way you have.
We all have to grow up sometime.

I've never been allowed tay 'grow up'.
I'm trapped here. In this cell. In this *state*.
Vegetating. Kept captive, alive, and for whit?
Observation? Experimentation?

Paranoid.

Are you takin samples when I sleep?
Drawin blood. Slicin me open?
Whit have ye tane?
Ma kidneys? Ma liver?

Not that they'd be upto much.

Aye, it's nae wunner I take a drink.

So it's the 'wasn't me' defence, is it?
An older boy did it and ran away.
Big Bad England, bending you to its will,
just forcing you into all those countries

275

to turn the brown-skinned people
into your slaves.

You didn't want to do it!
You had a bad childhood!

You still took the money though.

What did you spend it on?

Let's have a look, shall we?

                                    Whaur are we gawin?

Come on.
Now, where are we?

                                    Glesga.

Very good. How can you tell?

                                    Cos I seem to be...drunk.

Oh god.

                                    (sings)
                            I belong tay Glasgow
                            Dear old Glasgow toon.
                    But there's something the matter wi Glasgow.
                            Cos it's goin roun and roun.
                        I'm only a common workin chap,
                                    And that's-

Yes very good. Have you met this
other common working chap?

                                    He's a statue.

Well, give him time, the pubs aren't open yet.
Duke of Wellington.
Commander in Chief of the British Army.
Twice Tory Prime Minister.
Put the Hindus to the sword
on behalf of the British East India Company.
And Glasgow has built him a monument.

> Ah, but see that traffic cone on his heid?
> That's what Glaswegians really hink ay him.

Glassford Street, Buchanan Street,
Ingram Street, Oswald Street.
How do you think they got their names?

> Somebody stuck a pin in a phone book?

Tobacco Lords.
Men whose wealth came from the plantations,
Men who lived like princes.
You see this splendid architecture all over the city?
All paid for by the broken backs of slaves.

> East End. Highest poverty levels in Europe.
> Food banks. Knife crime.
> That tobacco wealth didnay exactly spread, did it?
> At the height ay the Empire maist ay the folks in this city
> steyed in slums.

Paisley Road. Taking us towards Ibrox,
See these proud, fluttering Union Jacks?
How difficult do you think things
were made for Catholic immigrants…?

> Fenian bastarts.

What's that?

Red Clydeside.
Workers standin up against the might and brutality ay capitalism.
Then, later, Glasgow was the first city in the world tay offer Nelson
Mandela its freedom,
when the British government
were still condemning him as a terrorist.

FREEEEEEDOM!

Right, son, you just sit there and sober up, eh?

(*sings*)
Glasgow…concrete jungle where dreams are made of,
There's nothin ye can't do.
When ye're in Glasgow…Glasgow…Glasgow…

Ken how they say the Eskimos have fifty words for snow?
I've got fifty for the drink.
The boattle. The bevy.
A dram. A hauf. A swally. A sesh.
Doolally. Mashed. Mad wae it. Oan a bender. Wrecked.
Oan the lash. Pished. Steamboats.
Blotto. Stocious. Oot ma box. Oot ma nut.
Fucked. Havin a scoop. Blootered. Bladdered. Fu.
. Combined together they make a pissheid. A jakie. An alky.
A jalky (if ye're take it wi drugs).

You think I'm durty?
She thinks I'm durty.

Well we've got plenty durty words for ye.
Clatty. Clarty. Mockit. Hackit.
Cleggit. Hingin. Mingin. Honkin.
Gien me the boak. A mink. A tink. A coagie.
Manky. Skanky. Houfin. Boufin.
Dreich. Jobbies. Keech.

Whit does this mean?

A country whit makes a lexicon ay addiction,
whit makes poetry fay its ain effluence.
Is this the behaviour ay an affluent nation?
Or a trapped wan?

For aw that I helped rule the world,
and took and took and took,
I exhibit the pathetic traits ay the same colonies
that I helped oversee.
The Irish, Native Americans, the Aborigines:
alkies just like me.

I crushed the robust shape ay these territories
intay the same model as masel.
Wretched. Deferential.
Inconsequential.

How did this happen?

Jock says goodbye to his neighbours, puts on his tammy, marches South. He sets himself up on the throne, and George removes the tammy and crowns him with the bowler hat. He waves to his subjects

JUDGE (v-o) Calling character witness for the defence:, novelist, painter and author of *Why Scots Should Rule Scotland.*

GRAY By 1695 it was obvious to most Scots that having a king in London did not benefit them. The lords and gentry in Scotland's parliament could only deal with their ruler through a small number in the monarch's pay. Meanwhile, King Billy, and after him Queen Anne, signed English acts of parliament which strengthened English colonies, English trade and the English stock exchange in ways which excluded Scotland. English fleets traded with colonies and plantations containing Scottish overseers and settlers, but which excluded Scottish ships; nor could the Scots trade freely with Europe because England was usually at war with either Holland or France, her chief mercantile competitors. When James VI had gone south over ninetey years before he had told the Scots he was going from one part of an island to another to secure their comfort. The only folk made more comfortable had been some other clever émigrés who went south with him.

Jock wearing bowler hat, bored. He sits on the throne waves half-heartedly to people. He goes to the bin and takes out the tammy. Looks at it sadly. He tries it back on. It doesn't seem to suit him anymore. Then he gazes nostalgically back towards Scotland.

He holds the tammy in one hand, the bowler hat in the other. He's thinking carefully. Then he brings the two of them together. He's got it!

George arrives with a contract, entreating him to sing. Jock does so, then places both the tammy and the bowler hat on his head.

The police interrogation room.

GEORGE   **JOCK**

Admit it, you needed the money.

                    Why else does onybody turn tay crime?

Is that what you'd call the ceasing of hostilities
between two nations who'd opposed each other for
Four hundred years – a crime?

                    Wan ay many.

But a crime committed by yourself
against yourself.

                    Caw it self-harm.
          That's whit us sullen, fucked-up teenagers dae.

So who did you owe?

> You tell me. You've got the file right there.

The Darien Scheme:
an attempt by your merchant class
to establish a colony in Panama in the late 1690s.

> Cos yese had banned ma exports
> in an attempt tay strangle me.

This failed colony bankrupted you, causing you to seek Union with
your wealthier Southern neighbour.

> Seek Union?
> There were riots in the streets against it!

In return for shared access
to my trade routes

> Routes ye'd blocked me fay on purpose.

We generously paid off your Darien losses.

> Eywis check the small print.
> We had tay pey that 'compensation'
> back through oor Excise Duty.
> Meaning: yese bribed us wi oor ain money,
> while dumpin us with a share ay yer debt.

Our debt. We pool and share resources-

> Aye whose resources?
> I might be part ay a racket awright.
> But wha's runnin it?

Never read the McCrone Report, 1974?

Never heard of it.

A wee file yese've got on me that
ye never expected me tay read.
It concluded that were I to take
control of my own oil reserves
I would be one of the richest countries in the world.
But you. Wouldnay. Let me.

Obsessed with the past.

Leave the past whaur it is eh?

I wunner why.

You came to us bankrupt.
You flourished under Union.

It wasn't a Union!

What was it then?

It was a forced merger.
A hostile takeover.
A shotgun wedding.
I had power. Status. Autonomy.
Folk respected me.
Ye manipulated the chessboard til ye had me exactly
whaur ye wanted me
and then wi wan stroke ay the pen:
check mate.
Ye took it aw aff me.

Your psychatric evaluation has come back:
"Subject tells himself fantasies about his
own history to compensate for guilt about his crimes."
In short: you self-deceive to cover up for the fact that
you did this to yourself. Every step of the way you had options.
If this is what you've become it's because
you've chosen it.

(mad laughter)

Psychiatric conclusion: schizophrenia.

JUDGE (v-o) Calling character witness for the defence: Paul Henderson Scott, historian and author of *Still in Bed With An Elephant.*

HENDERSON SCOTT The Union of 1707 achieved a centuries-old objective for the English: to bring Scotland under control and remove a potential threat to their northern border.

To Scotland it meant the loss of the independence defended against heavy odds for over 300 years.

There'd been an uprisin.
The Jacobite claim denied, its body
booted up and doon Culloden. Bonnie Prince Charlie's
foolhardy plans for the throne dashed,
his followers dispersed like trash,
nowhere in the United Kingdom safe.

The haven of foreign shores sang
like mermaids. I made my merry way to India, America, the Carribean,
Canada and Australia,
South Africa – in conjunction wi ma new best pal- we made it oors.
Turned their women intay hoors,
their men intay slaves.

I'd watch them every day while I sipped a whisky,
picking at them fields,
sweatin intay the earth. How does it feel?
Chuckin yersel intay yer work
only for some ither bastard tay come by and tak whit's yours
like some monstrous dragon
poised there waitin for ye tay dae yer back in,
before it swoops and roars and takes yer gold,
tobacco, linen, minerals, sugar, pussy, dignity.

That's how the world is.
I learned this lesson the hard wey,
the Scottish wey: through sufferin.

Nae mair. I wid prove masel on the world stage.
Noo, thanks tay the UK, I wis a player.
Spare the rod and spoil the child,
That's whit they say.
Ye cannay have them runnin wild
through oor plantations.
I smell a revolution.

Pit them doon! Pit them aw doon!
Whip them! Hang them by their baws!
Naebody messes wi the Scots.
Tie them tae a cross. Chop aff their feet.
See how they run away noo. Hire some ay them
tay rule the ither yins, tae look doon on them,
Tae identify wi oor race, oor European grace,
Wi oor superior craniums and manners,
Make them feel inferior.
Inferior. Inferior!
Eat my feces,
Like the good sub-species that you are,
And most of all, do not forget
I am your High Commander,
Jock – your overlord.
Toil so I may thrive or else I'll throw you on a fire.
And by the sword of the mighty Britsh Empire
I sentence you to die die die die die!

JUDGE (v-o)   Calling character witness for the prosecution: Jackie Kay: novelist and poet.

KAY   At school, I learnt that Glasgow was a great merchant city. I learnt about the shipping industry, but not about the slave ship Neptune that arrived in Carlisle Bay, Barbados, on May 22 1731, after leaving Port Glasgow months earlier, carrying 144 enslaved Africans, half of whom were children. When they arrived they were "polished" – meaning a layer of skin was removed with fierce scrubbing – and a wadding rammed up the rectum of those who had dyssentery, and then put up for sale.

Scotland never acknowledges the Scottish plantation owners who were often as cruel as his English or American counterpart. It almost seems anti-Scottish to imagine all those MacDonalds out there in Jamaica stuffing their faces on mutton broth, roast mutton, roast goose, stewed mudfish and paw-paw, stewed giblets, fine lettuce, crabs, cheese, mush melon. Or knocking back punch, porter, ale, cider, Madeira wine and brandy – this from a true account of a plantation owner's meal in 1775 – while the enslaved Africans were whipped for sucking a sugar cane.

Police interrogation room. Jock is distraught.

GEORGE	JOCK

Are you alright?

It's aw comin back to me.

We're not so different.

Naw.

The question is:
What are you going to do about it?

Whit can I dae?

You can plead guilty.
Apologise to your victims.

Aye. I could do that.
It doesnay take the stain awa.

It helps.
Believe me, I know.
It helps.

I'll make the necessary arrangements.

One last hing.

Yes?

I want back whit's mine.

And what's that?

> Somethin that was taken fae me:
> Maself.

That'll be upto the decisions you make next.
You could always try banking?
Good luck.

Jock shakes hands with George. He leaves the police station and tries to hail a taxi. One passes him. Another passes him. He checks his watch. Never mind. There'll be another along soon. He looks hopeful. While this happens we hear:

JUDGE (v-o) Calling final character witness for the prosecution and the defence: Tom Johnston, historian and former Secretary of State for Scotland.

JOHNSTON We must show the people that our Old Nobility is not noble, that its lands are stolen lands – stolen either by force or by fraud; show people that the title deeds are rapine, murder, massacre, cheating or Court harlotry, dissolve the halo that surrounds the hereditary title; let the people clearly understand that our present House of Lords is composed largely of descendants of successful pirates and rogues; do these things and you shatter the Romance that keeps any nation numb and spellbound, while privelige picks its pocket.

Jacquoranda

A woman stands, shows a pill to the audience. Then she swallows it with a gulp of water and closes her eyes.

"No fags, no booze, no weed. How much more of it do you need?"

"No fags, no booze, no weed. How much more of it do you need?"

"No fags, no booze, no weed. How much more of it do you need?

(deep breath, opens eyes)

Welcome, friends. My name is Jacquoranda. But you may call me by my pure name: Jacquoranda.

I was once like you. I used to spend time in places like this, on my own. A bottle of wine. Maybe two? Standing outside in the cold and the rain, huddled, over a nicotine stick, and then home to skin up, and hide somewhere inside a cloud.

And I'm not going to lie to you, I had some good times. We do, don't we? Hen nights. Stag parties. Wedding receptions. Anniversaries. Hogmanay. Everything is just made easier with a drop of this stuff, isn't it? It's how we bond. As friends. As Scots.

But let me paint a picture for you. A child's birthday party. Boys and girls excitedly tearing the paper off presents. Pass the parcel! Musical statues! Fingers sticky with melted chocolate. And six drunk women in the kitchen, haranguing another woman about her dependence upon drink.

They were right to intervene. The difference between me and them is, I'm the only one now standing here, talking like this.

Friends, modern life has trapped us. Can't you feel it? Each of us getting up, going to work, coming home, housework, an hour of television or Facebook before bed, then you get back up and do it all again, like cogs in some vast, uncaring machine.

And how do we deal with it? Alcohol. Nicotine. Recreational drugs. Junk food. Sugar. Pornography. Consumerism. We are, each of us, slaves to our own addictions, lab rats experimenting on ourselves.

But I'm here to tell you how to break free of that, show you how to connect with the wellspring of life within, to bring more healing, peace, fulfilment into your life.

Now. I want one of you, friends, to do an experiment with me. You don't have to trust me. You only have to trust yourself.

(*to audience member*) Can I ask your name?

And what are you drinking (*name*)?

How much did it cost you?

Now, if someone was to say to you (*name*): I can give you the key to happiness for only (*price*), would you pay that?

I'm going to take this drink off you, and put it over here beside me. Would you let me do that (*name*)?

(*if says no*) That is your choice. Each of us exercises free will. But perhaps one day you'll realise the chance you've missed.
(*repeat until finds a willing audience member*)

Friends, please applaud (*name*). You just made a big step today. You are befitting of a pure name. (*hippy-dippy riff on audience member's name*).

That is exactly what happened to me when I met him. There I was, at the bar, trying to persuade the handsome, young barman to give me another. I just couldn't face going home to my husband and my children, to that pressure chamber, all its demands, its expectations: fill the dishwasher, lift the toys, cook the meals, wash the clothes, dry the clothes, hoover the floor, clean the windows til they sparkled. I couldn't take it anymore. I felt like an appliance the kitchen had bought.

I was staring into my fourth large glass of wine, when he sat down at the bar stool next to me. He spoke in his soft, clear voice. He said, 'Friend, you are lost.'

Of course, ladies, we're all used to such approaches by men in bars. Or, I certainly used to be. But there was something different about him. He only wanted me to talk. He only wanted to listen. Occasionally he would interrupt with a gentle, 'That must be difficult for you,' or 'Tell me more.' I wasn't used to anyone really hearing me. The more I spoke, the lighter my soul started to feel. His gaze held me up the way a father holds up a baby as it is learning to walk. I asked him his name. He smiled and said, 'Pear Tree'.

Then he did with me what I did with you (*name*). He asked if I would slide my wine glass over to him and let him be the 'custodian of my habit'. I was reluctant. Of course I was. I was addicted. But do you know how he persuaded me?

I'll show you. I would like everyone to raise their glass.

(*she also raises the glass she took from the audience member*)

Now. Close your eyes. Place the glass just under your nose. Whatever your drink is. Now breathe in its smell. If it is wine or whisky, then try and detect the flavours, sense its delicacy. If you have a beer in your hand, then allow the hops or the barley to unfold.

Now touch the glass to your lips and take a small mouthful, but do not swallow. I want you to imagine that this is the last mouthful of alcohol you will ever taste. The last in your lifetime. Savour it. Let it pool around your tongue. Explore the flavour of it. Explore the wetness of it in your mouth. Now swallow.

(*She drinks half the glass*)

Did you enjoy that? Of course you did. You sought the pleasure in it.

Now take another small mouthful. Again, feel it there in your mouth. This time, I want you to think of it is as…poison. Feel how sharp it is, how toxic. Taste the bitterness beneath it. Think of it eroding your liver and your kidneys. Think of tomorrow's hangover, how bleary and weak you will feel. Now remember, every single mouthful like this brings you closer to death.

Swallow.

(*She drinks the other half of the glass, and a brief, suppressed pleasure crosses her face. She holds up the empty glass*)

This is what Pear Tree told me I must become: an empty glass. Not a full glass, sloshing around with madness. But pure, clear, cradling the air. By the end of the evening it is what each of us will have become.

Those drinks on your table? You will not touch them for the remainder of the evening. Trust yourselves. Allow me to become the custodian of your habit.

(*She takes a couple of the audience's drinks and places them next to herself*)

And as I slid my wine glass down the bar towards Pear Tree, he smiled in that kind way he does and said, 'You are no longer Jacqueline. You are now…Jacquoranda.'

(*She receives a text*)

Excuse me.

(*Takes out her phone, looks at it, and there is a tiny moment of discomfort. She puts it away, and smiles at the audience*)

Sorry, my husband has not quite taken my…enlightenment…in his stride.

Let's press on, shall we?

Now that we have taken our last mouthful of poison, we have made an implicit promise to ourselves not to abuse our bodies, not to reject the power each of us has brewing within us, not to deny ourselves our essential humanity, and so we are now going to the Good Place, to that heavenly place, where we can forever be in touch with ourselves.

Again, close your eyes.

(*once everyone's eyes are closed, she lifts another of the drinks. As she delivers this speech, she pauses to drink every so often*)

You are on a tranquil beach. Feel the warm sunlight on your face. Hear the distant hiss and ebb of the waves, the chiming laughter of children. You have no work today, or ever. You have to be nowhere but here. No-one expects anything from you. Perhaps you have a beautiful partner beside you. It does not have to be your husband and wife, since these are often the people who bring us stress. It can be someone from your past, with whom you wish you'd never lost contact. It can be someone you've never met, but whose company you have always craved so, *so* much.

Reach across. Touch their hand. A gentle, human squeeze.

Open your eyes

(She has finished the drink. The audience see her replacing it to the table)

How did that feel? Good. Each of us is one step closer to ourselves. Let's share our pure names.

(To audience member) What's your name?

And what shall we call *(name)*?

(Takes suggestions. They arrive at a name. Repeat this with another audience member. During this period, we should start to notice Jacquoranda's accent change. She becomes broader, earthier, slightly saltier in her interaction with audience)

Now, I want everyone here to think of their pure name. Have you got one? Think. Hold it in your head. And on the count of three, we are all going to shout our new names at the same time. Are you ready? One... two...three...

(audience shout)

Again!

(audience shout)

Louder!

(audience shout)

Yes! Yes! You feel that? You feel that energy in the room! All those selves commingling together at once in the air. Doesn't it make you feel like a child tearing through a field, the grass tickling your bare calves, the breeze in your face. Yes! Yes! Our pure names are running free! We are becoming as one with each other. Now, say it with me:

"No booze, no fags, no weed. How much more of these things do we need?"

"No booze, no fags, no weed. How much more of these things do we need?"

"No booze, no fags, no weed. How much more of these things do we need?"

Good. Good. We are gradually losing our attachments.

(*Her phone rings. She cuts it off with a brief look of irritation*)

These are the steps I went through with Pear Tree. From that first moment in the bar, where he watched me take my last shot of poison, we went to his hotel room. The Premier Inn. Premier. As though I was first. He encouraged me to be naked, both spiritually and literally, and then he...stroked my skin. He planted soft kisses all over me. He told me he would make me reborn. When he entered me with his...fucking great dick...I felt cleansed. I felt new. I felt that I could never go home again.

Just as Pear Tree did this for me, so will I – Jacquoranda – do this for you.

I want you to turn and look at the person you have come here with.

(*As everyone does this, she picks up another drink, sips while she makes this speech*)

Hold them in your gaze. Look at their kind eyes. Their mouth. Their skin. Their hair. See how human they are. Think about what it is to love that person. Their best self, taking care of yours. Do you see their light? Now, look at me.

When next you see your partner, I want you to see something else. Turn to them. See their capacity for evil. See the cruelty beneath their gaze. Think of the lies they have told with that mouth. Think of the ways in which they might have hurt people, cheated. Think of how they might hurt you. Think of the thoughts like sewage cascading around in their head. Think of the ways in which they are holding you back in your life. How much stronger you would be without them. You are too dependent upon them. They do not care for you more than they care for themselves. Like the alcohol, they are poison.

(She drains the drink, holds it up)

The empty glass. Become the empty glass.

You do not need them. You do not need anyone. None of us *needs* anyone. What we need is already in here *(taps chest)*.

"And I think it's gonna be a long, long time / Til touchdown brings me around again to find / I'm not the man they think I am at home / Oh no no no...I'm a rocket man."

(She stares, lost in her own thoughts for a few seconds)

Everyone, come on. Come on! Outside!

(she leads everyone outside the pub)

Look at the sky. Do you see those stars? Each one of them billions of light years away, and yet here we are connected with them, us with our tiny, finite lives.

When I was a child, my father used to hold me in a tartan shawl and show me the stars. The constellations. The Big Dipper. The Great Bear. The Plough. My neck would get sore from looking up. Cradled there in his big arms. Singing to me, "Rocket man! Burning down the fuse up here alone."

(*She sings sadly to herself*)

"And I think it's gonna be a *long*, long time…And I think it's gonna be a *long*, long time…And I think it's gonna be a *long*, long time…"

That was before he went.

Breathe. Breathe. The air. The clean texture of it. You feel it? The purest thing in the world. Everyone close your eyes again. Breathe in. Now hold it there. Feel the power of your lungs. How full they are with that beautiful air, the stuff of life. Hold it there. Now slowly release. Enjoy the release. The relief of it. And before you breathe back in, hold it. That moment, that pregnant pause when you're breathing neither out nor in. The body at rest. Satisfied. For a few seconds. That oxygen making its way, into the bloodstream, making it rich, feeding your arteries, your heart, making it thump. Then breathe in again, slowly. Fill your lungs. Let your lungs be greedy for that air. Let them gorge themselves. Let them be their fullest. Feel the pressure. Then release slowly. The joy of it. And again, that pause. Like a shoreline, poised between the tide coming in and the tide going out. How pure the body feels. Again.

In…

Out….

Rest…

In…

Out…
Rest…

The tide advances…

The tide withdraws.

The sand waits...

The tide advances...

The tide withdraws...

The sand waits....

And the moon makes it all possible.

Now. Who here is a smoker? Ah. Could I please have a cigarette.

And do you have a light? Thank you.

Now see how the air changes.

(Sucks on cigarette, holds it there in her lungs, releases smoke. Again, barely suppressed pleasure)

You smell that? You see how dirty it makes the air, how polluted? You feel that acrid smell in your nostrils?

Disgusting.

(again, she takes a draw, holds it, releases)

My god, it's burning my lungs. It's corrupting them. Instead of clean, pure air going in, the body chokes, passing pollution into the blood, coating the lungs with tar, thickening the arteries.
(in, out)

I do this so you don't have to.

(in, out)

Directed not by the moon, but multinational tobacco companies, creating then exploiting our addictions.

(in, out)

My god. It's so, so bad.

The final cigarette I ever had was with Pear Tree. We were leaning out of the hotel window after we'd made love, after I'd ascended. And he told me about the daughter he never sees. He told me about the wife he left behind on his search for peace. I smoked a cigarette, happy to have my turn listening to him, feeling his pain make shapes in the smoke, but then – quite abruptly – he grabbed the half-finished cigarette and threw it to the ground.

(she throws the fag to the ground and stamps on it)

'You no longer need it,' he said. And he was right. He was right. We don't need these things. Pear Tree told me I should quit my job in the bank, leave my husband and family, and join him in bringing enlightenment to the world.

He pays for these courses because he believes *so much* in spreading inner-happiness. He recognised my gifts as a teacher and encouraged me. He brought me out of myself. He made me talking to you like this possible. I could never have done this in my old life. Public speaking? I wouldn't have had the confidence! Pear Tree pays for my travel, my accomodation and your ticket money goes back to him to help him liberate the people of Scotland from their negative habits.
Isn't that wonderful?

Let's go back inside.

(She leads everyone back in. On the table are paper and pens)

Now. I want everyone to write down one thing that they have learned so far.

(She waits while they do so, then collects the paper and reads them aloud. She rolls with the answers here, eliminates the negatives, accentuates the positives)

So, clearly some of you are on the path to enlightenment. But some of you are still stuck in your old ways. How sad.

(Her phone rings. She picks it up and looks at it, smiles).

It's Pear Tree everybody!

Hello? Yes! Pear Tree!

Pear Tree says hi!

Everyone says hi, Pear Tree.

Yes, it's going really well! I've really made a breakthrough with some of them. Yes, we've done the breathing exercises, looked at the stars, repeated the mantra, and we're ready to proceed to the next stage. You'd be proud of them, you really would.

He says to remember each of you have an inner god or goddess.

Everyone says 'We know, we know…' Ha ha.

(she winks at audience)

What? Have I had a drink? Of course I haven't. That's not part of the programme, why would I have had a drink? Yes I know, but I've never done that since, have I?

Of course I took their cigarettes off them. And put them all in the bin, yes.

Yes. I'll get the last train home. I won't stay out. It was a one-off, I told you. No. I understand the discipline. Yes, okay. Bye. Love y-

(*he's hung up*)

Pear Tree says remember your breathing.

He's *so* disciplined.

Such a good teacher.

(*Something seems to move inside her head and her chest. She stops in her tracks, smiles*)

Oh.

Oh.

It's happening.

(*grins*)

Pear Tree taught me how to discover nirvana. The breathing. The abstinence. I'm not going to lie to you, it's difficult sometimes. Takes a lot of work. *So* much work. Demands a lot from you, y'know.

Sometimes you can't be bothered.
Something you just want a…shortcut.

In pill form.

Oh yes.

Oh yes.

Look at my fingers! Look at them? Aren't they great? Let me see your fingers.

Wow. Your hands are really elegant. You are ageing really well. No, I know nobody likes having their ageing acknowledged, but let's face it we're all ageing, aren't we. No use pretending otherwise. We're all ageing and we're all going to die one day…and that's okay.

We lived.

Us. Here. Together. Now. Sharing this universe. This planet. This country. At this time in history. In this room. That's so…special.

I love all of you.

Do you love me?

Do you love me?

You do? You do! Of course you do! Love is what we are made from. Our mothers and fathers met, like two atoms in space, they collided, and their love for each other made each of us. We are all the same. We are made from the same materials. We experience the same emotions – envy, fear, jealousy, rage, happiness, excitement and love. And yet, like individual snowflakes, we are all different in tiny ways. Unique ways. Each of us is the same, but each is unique.

I love the colour of your hair. You have beautiful eyes. Your laughter lines are to die for. Don't be ashamed of them. They're what makes you

you. Don't be ashamed of getting older, anyone. We were born and then we live and then we die. Rich, poor, black, white, fat, thin….all of us die. It's so…it's so…fair.

Everyone. Place your hand on your heart. Feel it beating? You are alive. You have that gift. Never, ever waste it. Whenever life feels as though it is defeating you, place your hand on your heart and feel that pulse and say: I exist. I exist. Against the odds, life has happened on this planet and you have been created with a consciousness to reflect upon your existence. You are not an amoeba. You are not a spider. You are not a dog. You are a human, awake and sentient.

B-doom. B-doom. B-doom.

(*The thump of house music starts. She hears it, feels it. It gets louder. She stands on the table. Louder. She strips off her top, down to her bra, whoops like a raver, whirls her top around her head, throws it into the audience. Then she dances, not sexually, just enjoying the pure joy and flexibility of her body. She is free. She is free! No-one is telling her what to do. She is beyond the control of everyone. Does she even liberate people from the audience and get them to dance with her? If they won't, she doesn't care. It's their choice! Her body moves, writhes, at one with the music, and then it stops-*

The barman/maid declares that it is too loud. And that no dancing is allowed on the table. She hops off the table, runs towards the bar and kisses him/her, giggling)

Ah. Full flow.

Severed

(*Cocksure, confident, the ecstacy flowing through her. She does all of the following smiling, or ironically, as though she's in on some vast, cosmic joke*)

Now this brings us to the last stage of our wee group therapy session.

We've conquered alcohol. We've conquered relationships. We've conquered nicotine. We've conquered recreational drugs. Ha ha ha HA HA HA HA!

What's left? What's left? (*fields suggestions from audience*)

That's right. The final fig-leaf. Sex.

"Let's talk about sex, bay-bee / Let's talk about you and me / Let's talk about all the good things and the bad things that may be."

Let's talk about sex.

Put your hand up if you've had sex.

(*goes to someone who doesn't have their hand up. There's bound to be one*)

You've never had sex? But you just said you hadn't. Would you like to have sex?

No! (*does exaggerated denial pose*) No. We can't do that. It's not allowed. It's not in the rules. Discipline is what's required! That didn't stop Pear Tree OBVIOUSLY from taking me that night, but since then I have learned that what's in his plan is…

Abstinence.

Abstinence! Like a bottle of green alcohol. Abstin…cence?

This is what he said to me. He said, 'If you can touch the flame then withdraw your hand. If you can bring yourself so achingly close to fulfilment and then deny yourself. If you can desire and not act. If you can keep your head when all about are losing theirs and blaming it on you if you can trust yourself when all men doubt you but make allowance for their doubting too yours is the EARTH and everything that's in it and which is more you'll be a MAN my son.'

You'll be a man, my son.

Ha.

A man.

(*approaches best looking man in the room*)

Hi.

You married?

You married to her?

(*if yes*) Yeah? (*to woman*) You're very lucky. Can I kiss your husband? On the lips? No? Did you not hear what I said earlier about us all being one and made of atoms and all that. What's a kiss between human beings? (*if woman doesn't object she kisses the man so passionately*) Shh. Don't tell Pear Tree. (*if woman objects*) If you were up here, where I am, you wouldn't object. You'd get it. It's not your fault. I respect you.

(*if not with a partner, kisses the man passionately*) Shh. Don't tell Pear Tree.

I didn't have sex. So it's all right.

(*gets a text*)

Oh. I've got a text. Do you want to hear it?

Okay, who remembers Jackanory? Man, I used to love Jackanory. Storytime. Let's have Storytime! Come round and sit on the floor. Come on!

(*She gets everyone to sit on the floor in front of her. She takes on the role of a storyteller*).

Now. Are we sitting comfortably? Then we'll begin.

(*she reads out text*)

"Stop this nonsense and come home at once."

Well.

Well well well.

(*she throws the phone away*)

Never mind Jackanory. It's time for Jacquoranda.

I'll tell you a story.

Once upon a time there was a girl, born poor. And they promised her the world. Her Daddy showed her the stars and told her that everything could be hers. But her Daddy would not last forever and her Mummy was weak and the girl found herself alone in the world. Then she met a handsome Prince, who promised to take care of her and love her, but instead imprisoned her in a castle. There the girl stayed for years, pining, looking after the Prince's children, until one day a magician entered the castle. He cast a spell that liberated the girl and made it possible for her to fly. She flew away from the handsome Prince and followed the magician as he turned trees to gold and made rivers into rainbows. Together they enchanted the land. They went from village to village, the girl oohing and aahing as the magician cast his spells, encouraging the villagers to throw away their chains. The divine right of kings and princes, the villagers realise, is unfair.

But then something happens. The girl wonders why the magician gets to be the one who casts the spells. He tells her this. His face arranges itself in a downcast way, and she is reminded of the Prince, but only briefly. The magician gives her his wand, shows her how to cast the spells. But there are rules attached. The magic words must be intoned like so. The wand must be waved like so. She follows the rules. She goes round the village. She casts the spell.

Then she senses the power of the wand. She wants to create spells of her own. The magician senses an insurrection. He asks for the wand back. She says no. He uses his magic power against her, and she resists, but only for so long.

Only for so long.

(sings)

And I think it's gonna be a long, long time. / Til touchdown brings me round again to find / I'm not the man they think I am at home.

Oh no no no…I'm a rocket man.

Rocket man! Burning down the fuse up here alone.

And I think it's gonna be a long, long time.

And I think it's gonna be a long, long time.

And I think it's gonna be a long, long time....

The Incredible Adam Spark

Alan Bissett

adapted from his novel

Thunderclap!

Theme music!

The Incredible Adam Spark flies through the air. Famous landmarks whizz past: Eiffel Tower, Sphinx, Statue of Liberty, Taj Mahal. The Falkirk Wheel. He heads downwards. People point and gasp as he flies overhead. Adam salutes them. There's a robbery! He lifts the villains into the air, drops them outside the police station, dusts his hands. The police wave. There's a cat stuck up a tree! Adam uproots the tree and shakes the cat out, tousles the little boy's hair. An old woman comes out and finds her tree uprooted, shakes her fist at him. Adam perches atop the Steeple on the High Street, surveys the land he has sworn to protect.

V-O   This world has few heroes left.

All around we see crime, injustice, chaos. Who will defend the weak, if not the strong? Who will defeat the selfish needs of men, if not the virtuous and true? Because there are those...those *cowards* ... who would use their powers for gain, for evil.

But not this man.

Not, my young friends, The Incredible Adam Spark.

You have heard legends. You have heard tales of his bravery, his might. Perhaps you are aware of the time when he defeated the Tammy-Hill Young Team, single handed. Their Buckfast breath as he held them at bay, their chibs pressed against his throat. Maybe you have heard of the famous McChicken Sandwich Incident? She brought it back to the counter, said there wasn't enough pickle. He gave her some more pickle.
The legends are true.

He was sent from a far-off place, remote from the ken of mortal man. A fantastic, magical place. A place called... Falkirk.

And he was sent to save a world in turmoil, in chaos. A world that can no longer tell the difference between right and wrong. A world that needs to be

Jude   tidied up, would you look at this mess? I telt you to get this room cleaned, Adam! Right. C'mon. Move.

Adam   Aye awright, Judy, awright.

Jude   And hurry up and get yer costume sorted. The parade'll be comin past the now.

Adam   Jeezo what's ma sister like when she's on her peeeeeriod man, sweartay god. And by the way, only Judy gets to call me Adam. Don't you be calling me that, man, cos to you I'm Sparky. Sparky! Like an electric shock dzzt.

Ow!

Jude   How do I look?

Adam   Depends. Who ye meantay be?

Jude   Wonder Woman.

Adam   Em, the costume, Judy. No think ye're mibbe a wee bit... well (*makes a bloater face*)

Judy   Oh. Thanks, Adam.

Adam   Whoops dudes! Think I pissed her off a teensy tiny wittle bit!

Gonnay fix ma cape, Judy? Trippin me at the back.

And ma mask keeps slippin off...

And these tights keep riding up ma-

Jude   Adam, you're gonnay have to start doin a lot more for yourself. I cannay be there all the time. No all the time.

Adam   (*pause*) How where ye goin, like?

Jude   Okay. Better?

Adam   Needtay be. So, Judy, think there'll be any crime for me to foil at the Gala Day?

Jude   Aye. There's karaoke on in the Glen Club.

Adam   Maybe I can use my ultrasonic hearin to detect some villainy...

Jude's mobile rings

Adam   Got somethin!

Jude   Hello. Oh hi, Maryann. You still coming through from Glasgow for the Gala Day?

Adam   ...I'm pickin up...plans being made. A meetin?

Jude   Oh. Well. I'll just get you outside the uni library? Should be finished up in Falkirk by six.

Faint sound of children in distress.

Adam   ...screams. Children. There's a evil afoot, dudes...

Jude   For the fancy dress? My Wonder Woman outfit. Oh yes, I'm sure you would...

Adam   ...the innocent...they'll be hurt...

Sound of children screaming rises.

Jude   Wonder Woman carries a lassoo, remember? And you know what that can be used for...?

Adam   Jude, Jude, somethin's comin. Somethin big.

Jude   I think the parade's about to pass us, Maryann, so I'd better go. You too, baby. Ciao.

Jude   Jude, look it's here! It's here!

Screaming becomes children laughing, cheering. Fairground noises. Music.

Jude   Aye okay, Adam, I'm comin.

They start to march. Adam's holding a big Scotland flag.

Adam   Hallglen gala day's the best day of the year, dudes!

Always sunny. Roastin. Boilin. Boof!

We all march march march to the big grass park down at the Glen Club. And there's a celebrity who says 'I now pronounce you the Hallglen Gala Day Queen.' And sometimes the celebrity's a cool deejay off Central FM ooooooor

the MP for Falkirk West

ooooooor

Kelly Marie off River City.

Kelly Marie off River City?!

And the queen well she touches her crown, goes, 'As queen I promise to help the good people of Hallglen.' And the good people of Hallglen? They cheer. Raay! There's loadsay races games shows crisps sweets juice and folk peeing behind the tents psshhhhhh. Shake shake. Cos see the Glen Club? They won't let them use their toilets.

There's an egg n spoon race:

Go.

Ye dropped it.

Ya tool.

Too cool for cats man, sure is. There's a fancy dress prize! And me and Jude's *totally* gonnay win it! Cos see her? See ma big sister? She's ma best pal. *She's* not gonnay disappear off to Oz now, is she dudes? No siree! Me and her's gonnay be together forev-

Animalz   Well look who it is.

Mongol boy.

And his lesbian sister.

Adam   O jobbies. The H-Glen Animalz. Talk about supervillains!

Animalz   Hey we like yer costumes.

Very smart.

Who yese meantay be?

Adam   I'm The Incredible Adam Spark and she's em Wonder Woman.

Animalz   Woman?

I wonder!

Jude slow claps.

Jude   Yese doin a turn at the gala day boys?

Animalz   Whit was that?

Jude   Think yese are funny, like? Think yese are hard? Mon then, I'll take yese the now.

Animalz Whatever.

Dyke.

Adam Hulk smash!

Jude Aye I will, Adam. Ma fist right intay their wee muppet faces.

Adam Cmon, Judy. No wantin to miss the fancy dress prize eh? Corry-nay-shin of the queen and that?

Animalz Lesbo.

Jude Och, piss off.

Adam Whit does that mean, Judy? Whit's a Lesbo?

Jude Um. Eh. The Mighty Lesbo. She's a…superhero.

Adam That right? Never hearday her. Never hearday Mongol Boy either, right enough.

Jude Wheest, Adam.

Adam Mongol Boy and The Mighty Lesbo! To the rescue!

Jude …Adam, folk can hear ye…

Adam We'd better get a move on, Judy. Will we take the Mongol-bike or the Lesmobile?

Jude Shut up. *Shut up.* Stop usin that word ya stupid-

Adam	Oh.
	Oh Judy.
	You. Said…
Jude	Adam. I'm sorry. I didn't meantay
Adam	…you called me…
Jude	Look. I mean. It's that lot. They just wind me up, ken?
Adam	…no ma fault…
Jude	I ken. I'm sorry, Adam.
Adam	…Mam never usedtay call me…
Jude	C'mon, Adam. Em. Listen. Let's win the fancy dress prize eh?
Adam	(*stares*)
	Aye.
	Aye!
	Let's win the fancy dress prize!
	C'mon Judy. Run! Run run run run run! Let's win the fancy dress prize! Oyah beezer, let's win the fancy dress prize! And ye'll never guess what, dudes? Ye'll never guess what happens? Oyah beezer man, ye'll never guess what happens next!

We comes last.

So. We're standing watching the Merican fitba.

Ho-hum.

Why's there Merican fitba in Scotland man? The fitbas aren't even the right shape! Huh. Mericans are daft. Can make great films like Spider-Man Batman X-Men Hulk raaaargh. Cool! But cannay make fitbas?
The Hallglen Redskins are heading into the end-zone for a 6-yard touchdown run to make the score 42-30 with less than twelve minutes remaining.

The Polmont 49-ers have to connect in the fourth quarter if they wanna salvage the game.

It's a long throw from the quarterback straight towards the wide receiver!

He's weaving through.

Leaves two men trailing in his wake and...!

Oh jobbies.

This wee wean wanders ontay the park. This wee toddler. Right intay the middle of the action. And none of them notice. None of them see! His mammy screams eeeeeeeeeeeeeeeeee and I thinks

What would a hero do?

What would a hero do?

I HAVE THE POWER!

I runs ontay the park man. Dodging Merican fitba players – one two three. Biff! Bosh! Hut hut hut!

then the world goes slooooow.

Adam weaves this way, ducks that way. American footballers throw and catch in slow motion around him. He dashes in and out till he reaches the wean.

Got. To. Get. You. Out. Of. Here. Son. Too. Dang. Er. Ous. For. You. Come. On. Let's. Go. Wee. Man.

It all speeds up.

...ball comes flyin over and...

...two meaty Merican fitba players jumpin for it at the same time and...

...don't see us then...

BOOM!

Black.

Mother   Somewhere over the rainbow. Way up high...

Adam   Mam?

Mother   ...there's a land that I heard of, once in a lullaby...

Adam   Mam!

Jude switches on the light.

Jude   Ah. Ye're awake, Adam. Feelin okay?

Adam   Judy? Whit happened? Where am I?

Jude   Ye're at home. What were ye thinkin about? Runnin ontay the park with all them big guys chargin about?

Adam   Park? Whit?

Jude   The American fitba. Ye ran on after that wean earlier. At the Gala Day, mind? Ye've been oot cold for about an hour.

Adam   Wean. Aye. Is he alright?

Jude   He's fine. Could've went for another shot, I think! You took quite the wee bump though.

Adam   But I saved him?

Jude   Aye, Adam. Ye saved him.

Adam   Saved him.

Jude   (*kisses his forehead*) Look, I've gottay go.

Adam   Ye're leavin me? Here?

Jude   Ma seminar starts in an hour. Got to get all the way through to Glesga for it.

Adam   Aye. Okay.

Jude   Be back soon though. There's soup in the fridge if ye get hungry.

Adam   (*glum*) Thanks.

Jude   Adam. Ye've only got concussion, it's nothin serious. We've been through this before. I cannay miss seminars, not with ma Social Science exams comin up.

Adam   Ye meetin anybody special there, Jude?

Jude   Naw, Adam. It's a seminar. Who would I be meetin?

Adam   (*pause*)

          On ye go then.

Jude   (*pause*)

          There's different ways to be a hero, Adam.

Jude exits

Adam   A hero...?

His fingertips crackle, fizz.

          A hero...

Lights. Colour. Faint theme music.

          What's that, Mr Provost? Falkirk needs me? I hear you, sir. Like I hear the innocent voices of this town. The weans of Camelon. The bairns of Bonnybridge. The wee tykes of Tammyhill. The Incredible Adam Spark will save them from the...horrors of this world. So you just spark up the Sparky Signal, Mr Provost. Cos here I comes!

He flies off at top speed.

Lands in…

McDonalds.

Removes superhero costume. Into regulation crewcap, trousers and shirt. Starts mopping, whistling.

Angie   Results! That's what I expect in this place. Get them fries intay the pokes afore ye burn them like yer usual. Get them burgers on that grill. Move! If yer troosers had pockets I'd be tellin ye to take yer hands oot them. Ya lazy buncha bastards. Think this company makes its money from gettin clowns to wave at weans? Move!

And look who it is. Bright spark.

Adam   Hiya, Angie!

Angie   Ah'll hiya you. While we're on the subject of clowns, bright spark, guess whose name's in that accident book three times last week.

Adam   Oh. Em. Hang on. I'll get it.

Angie   Aye, you will get it.

Adam   Wait a minute, I'm sure I ken this one.

Angie   Didn't I warn you not to get lippy?

Adam   …on the tip of ma tongue…

Angie   DIDN'T I WARN YOU NOT TO GET LIPPY?

Adam	Nup. I give up. You'll just have to tell me who it is.
Angie	I'll tell ye, bright spark. Listen carefully. It was you.
Adam	Och, that's right. So it was! How could I forget?
Angie	Three times! And do ye ken what for?
Adam	You'll no catch me out this time, Angie. Hang on. Em. I dropped that box of burgers on Peter's foot?
Angie	Aye.
Adam	Left a spillage on the floor and Fiona slipped?
Angie	Uh-huh.
Adam	And...hm..... Let me think. Oh! I burnt Davy's hand with the rack of fries!
Angie	That's right, bright spark. Well done. Spot on.
Adam	Honest? Did I get it right! Oh c'mon, Angie, ye cannay argue with that. All three guesses correct?
	Aye ye cannay beat Sparky in the old quiz stakes likes. And see cos I'm goin for employee of the month? Passin that wee test is sure to get me intay Angie's good books. So put me down for one heckuva good start to the day!
	She moves me from moppin duties to rackin the fries.
Grill	Drop five pans of fries into the fat.
Adam	I'm on the case, Mr Grill.

Fry me a river!

Grill   Scoop up the cooked fries.

Adam   Got it, Mr Grill.
Fry me to the moon and let me play among the stars. Let me see what fries are like on Jupiter and Mars.

Grill   Place the end of the scoop into the poke. Make sure those fries are standing up, Adam. Straight up.

Adam   Got it, Mr Grill. Come fryyyy with me!

Wouldya like to go large, sir?

Aye, me and Mr Grill here we make a good team, don't we, Mr Grill?

Grill   Shut up. Keep working.

Adam   Ha ha. See this company, man? They demand per-feck-shun. Like Angie says. Otherwise they wouldn't be as big and famous and well-loved by all the Falkirk kiddywinkles.

Hey Falkirk kiddywinkles!

Wean   Hiya Sparky! Wantay play hopscotch?

Adam   Sure thang. I'm a syooperb hopscotcher me like, the dude, the boy Sparky.

Hop skip hop skip.

Door opens creeeeeeeak. Like a vampire waking, the wean's mam appears.

Wean's Mam Manda. What've I telt ye about talkin to strangers?

Wean But Mam, Sparky's no a stranger. He lives in oor street.

Wean's Mam Aye well that's no the point. And you, Sparky. What do ye think ye're playin at?

Adam Hopscotch.

Wean's Mam Lessay yer cheek. Ye shouldn't be playin with wee weans at your age. Ye ken what folk are gonnay think?

Adam Aye. Folk'll think me and Manda's pals.

Whit's the problem, dudes? Why does I get this wherever I goes? Whit do folk look at me like that for? Whit do they want? Should I do a wee dance mibbes? An Irish jig or somethin? Whit dae they stare at me for, why's everybody always *starin* at me for? Eh? Eh? EH?

Judy!

Judy Whit is it now?

Adam Why do they stare at me like that for?

Judy Wheesht for a second, Adam, eh? Tryin to watch the news.

News As Allied forces prepare to attack, Tony Blair has said he won't wait for a Second UN resolution on the legality of the invasion. President Bush meanwhile said in a press conference that this was a war between good and evil, and that the US would stand strong on the side of-

Judy   Aye. Looks like war in the Gulf.

Adam   Can I watch The Wizard of Oz?

Judy   I think this is mair important, Adam.

Adam   Is Mam in the Gulf?

Judy   Whit? Naw. Course no.

Adam   It's no mair important then.

Jude   Adam. Listen. About Mam. Let me explain this to ye one mair time.

Adam   Somewhere over the rainbow...way up high....

Jude   Stop that. Listen. I'm tryin to talk to you, Adam.

Adam   ...there's a land that I heard of once in a lullaby....

Jude   She's not in Oz, Adam, she's-

Adam   THERE'S NO PLACE LIKE HOME. THERE'S NO PLACE LIKE HOME. THERE'S NO PLACE LIKE-

Jude   Okay! Okay Adam, shh. It's fine. Shh. She's in Oz. Mam's in Oz.

Adam   Can I go there?

Jude	Yes, Adam. You can go there. One day.
Adam	Can we watch the film again?
Jude	*(sighs)* Aye. I'll set up the DVD. Why don't you go and get some munchies from the shop eh?
Adam	The pakis?
Jude	Telt you before Adam, stop using that word. That's no a nice word.
Adam	But that's the name of the shop. That's whit everybody calls it.
Jude	So? You don't like it when folk call ye retard, do ye? Ye don't like it when they call ye spastic?
Adam	Naw. But I don't mind if they call me paki!
	So aaaaanyway. Heads on overtay the pakisho-
	Overtay the shop.
	Hey, Mrs Akram!
Mrs Akram	Hi, Sparky, how are you today? Ah, I see you're wearing your Queen t-shirt. I like it. Looks good. Work it, brother.
Adam	Best band there's ever been, dudes!
Mrs Akram	I love that one...how does it go...*Don't stop me now...* What's it called?
Adam	Don't Stop Me Now?

Mrs Akram That'll be the one. I saw them live, you know. Wembley Stadium. '86.

Adam Woah! You saw Queen? Did you do the handclaps to Radio Gaga?

Mrs Akram Radio Goo-goo.

Adam Radio Ga-ga!

Together Radio what's new…? Someone still loves you…

Adam Who though? Who still loves me?

Mrs Akram Sorry?

Adam Never mind. Just a song. Suppose.

Mrs Akram I heard about your accident at the gala day, Sparky. Are you alright? Concussion, was it?

Adam Oh I've no time to be worrying about that, Mrs Akram. No with this war in the Gulf carry-on.

Mrs Akram Aye, it's a terrible business. But Saddam has to be stopped, Sparky. They should've got him the last time. Dragged him right out of that Imperial Palace of his and made him apologise to the families of all those people that he killed.

Adam Imperial palace? That mean he's got, like, Imperial Stormtroopers!

Mrs Akram Well, he has his royal army, yes.

Well   Ach, well this'll be nae sweat. Never seen Imperial Stormtoopers in action? If they're no missin Han Solo from five yards, they're bangin their heads offay spaceship doors.

Mrs Akram Ha ha, Sparky. Quite.

Adam   Doof!
Mrs Akram Ha ha ha ha.

Adam   Whit's she laughin at?

Whit *youse* laughin at?

Why's everybody always.

Laughin.

Everytime I opens ma.

Mooth.

Comedian round here or somethin, dudes?

If so.

Then hey.

Mr Comedian.

Whit's brown and sticky?

A stick.

Ha ha, you thought it was gonnay be jobbies, ya dirty buncha

H-Glen Animalz enter.

Animalz   Alright Sparky.

How's it goin?

Good pals youse two, aren't yese?

Suppose yese make a good match.

A daftie.

And a paki.

Dunno who to feel mair sorry for.

Mrs Akram That's enough of that from you boys. I told you before, I don't want you in my shop.

Animalz   Ye hearin that, Sparky?

Doesn't want ye in her shop.

Mrs Akram Sparky is okay. He is a good boy. Not like you. Troublemakers. Now out. Leave.

Animalz   Ho.

Ho you.

Somethin against white people?

Ma brother's in Afghanistan.

Mine's goin to Iraq.

Cosay you and yer 9/11.

Lucky to be in this country.

Mrs Akram I am from Falkirk. I am not Taliban or al-Qaeda or friend of Saddam. Now go before I call the police.

Adam Dudes! See whit's happenin here? There's like this red light round the H-Glen Animalz heads and round Mrs Akram's it's dark blue. Whoah. Spoo-kee.

Animalz Aye well, we'll sort your lot out.

When we get intay Basra.

Ch-chk.

Boom!

That'll teach ye.

To go flyin planes intay buildins.

Ken whit we're sayin.

Adam's hands crackle and fizz.

Mrs Akram Right. That's it. Out of my shop now, go on.

Animalz Naw.

Adam stares at his hands. Looks from the Animalz to Mrs Akram. Hides his hands behind his back.

Adam   C'mon boys. (*laughs nervously*) I think she's had enough eh?

Animalz   Whit's that, Sparky?

Adam   Mibbe just leave it now, whit d'ye say?.
Animalz   Ye're defendin a Paki?

Against yer own people?

What's wrong with ye?

Adam   She's no a Paki. That word's not right.

Animalz   How would you ken?

The meanin of words.

Ya mongol.

Ya retard.

Paedo.

Mrs Akram   That's *enough*.

Adam   Whit does that mean, Mrs Akram?

Mrs Akram   It means you like weans, Sparky.

Adam   Whit's wrong wi that? I do like weans.

Animalz	Aye, *too* much.
Adam	The weans are ma pals. I'm no a lesbo.
Animalz	That's no whit he said.

He said paedo.

It's yer *sister* that's the lesbo.
Bet he doesnay ken whit that means either.

Means she cannae take the boaby.

She'd take *ma* boaby.

If she could find it!

Adam	Oh.

Don't.

Not Judy.

His hands are flaming with power.

Don't make me.

Animalz	Whit?
Adam	Don't make me angry.
Animalz	How no?
Adam	You wouldn't like me when I'm angry.

Animalz   That right?

Adam   With great power.

Animalz   Aye?

Adam   With great power comes.

Animalz   Whit?
Adam   Great responsiblity.

Animalz   The Incredible Adam Spark eh?

Adam   That's right.

Animalz gradually close in. Adam shrinks further and further from them.

Animalz   Listen.

Superhero.

Just watch.

Who ye're pickin fights with.

We'll let ye off this time.

Cosay you bein a *mongol* and that.

But talk tae us like that again.

And…

We'll…

Fuckin….

They roar! Adam yelps.

Mam   Wake up.

Adam   Mam?

Bedside lamp comes on.

Mam   Did ye have a bad dream, son?

Adam   I did Mam, aye.

Mam   Well, it's okay. I'm here with ye, wee man.

Adam   I ken ye are, Mam.

Mam   Know whit day it is the day?

Adam   Aye! It's Judy's birthday! Happy birthday to yooooooooo-

Mam   Shh. Don't wake her up. Wantay see whit I've got her?

Adam   Sure do, Mam! Sorry. I mean *(whispers)* Aye let's see.

Mam   Ta-dah!

Shows him a pair of red shoes.

Adam   Oh, they're byootiful. All sparkly n shiny, look at that.
             Like ruby slippers.

Mam   They're from Marks and Spencers.

Adam	She'll be like Dorothy, Mam. So pretty. Ooh I'm so excited!
Mam	Weren't cheap. But I just thought, well we've got to get her out of them army jackets and Doc Martens. No look for a young lady.
Adam	For somebody who hates the army, she sure does love them army jackets!
Mam	C'mon, let's go and surprise her.
Adam	Aye.
	Tip toe. Tip toe.
	Shh.
	(*Giggle*)
Mam	Ye ready?
Adam	Aye. (*Giggle*)
Mam	Okay?
	One...
	Two...
	Three...
Adam	Happy birthday, Judy!

Light comes up on Jude and Maryann, seated at a table.

Jude   Oh Adam, you finally made it.

Adam   (*Confused*) Yeah...

                Uh. Who's this?

Maryann   (*Stands to shake Adam's hand*) Hello, Adam. It's a great pleasure to meet finally you. I'm Maryann.

Adam stares down at her hand, but doesn't shake it

Adam   Hello, Maryann.

Jude   Maryann's a friend of mine from uni.

Maryann   I've heard a lot about you.

Adam   Cannay say the same.

Maryann   Well. I'm sure there are perhaps...reasons?...for that, Judith?

Adam   Judith? Only Mam called ye Judith. Didn't she, Judy?

Jude   She did, Adam, yes.

Uncomfortable silence.

Jude   Shall we have a look at the wine list?

Adam   Thought it was just going to be me and you for yer birthday?

Maryann   You didn't tell him I was coming?

Jude	(*whispers*) It's not as straightforward as that.
Adam	Know what I was just mindin, Maryann?
Maryann	Tell me, Adam.
Adam	Jude's birthday when I was wee.
Maryann	Aww.
Adam	Aye. It was just me, Mam and Jude.
Maryann	Mm.
Adam	Just. Us.
Maryann	Your father wasn't there at that point, Judith?
Judy	(*snorts*) My what?
Adam	And Mam had bought her these red shoes. Byootiful, they were.
Jude	I'm sure Maryann doesn't want to hear about that.
Maryann	No, I do. This is exactly why I was looking forward to meeting your brother. I want to hear all the stories from when you were a little girl. So. Tell me about the shoes, Adam. I bet she looked gorgeous in them.
Adam	Nah. She wouldnay wear them. Says it went against her. Whit wis the word, Judy…?
Jude	Principles.

Maryann	Ha ha. Always the radical, Judith. I mean, what's she like, Adam?

Adam	Oh, I ken!

Maryann	Ha ha. Oh, this is fun, you guys. I'm *so* glad to finally get the chance to speak to you, Adam. We're going to be *such* good friends.

She rubs his hand. He looks at it, then back up at her, stony.

So. No girly shoes for Judy, then?

Jude	No. That was Mam's doing. Always trying to get me into pigtails and make-up and bloody *frocks*.

Mother	Wear a frock, Judith.

Jude	She'd say.

Mother	It'll bring out yer eyes. Ye've got such adorable eyes, Judith.

Mother	She'd say.

Mum	Why don't you want to look like a girl?

Jude	I am a girl, Mum. I am a girl, therefore I look like one.

Mum	But, I mean a *nice* girl, Judith. Girls are supposed to be… well… fancier.

Maryann	Fancier?

Jude	Exactly.

Adam	She just wanted to spoil ye, Judy. Her wee lassie.
Jude	Every birthday, it was a 'party frock' and she'd invite these horrible girls from school, all of them immaculate as china dolls, just so she could show me off in my dress. And in they'd come in one by one and Mum would say
Mum	Aw look at her wee bunches!
	And whit's yer dolly's name?
	So whit are ye gonnay be when you grow up? An air hostess! Did you hear that, Judith. She's gonnay be an air hostess. And you'll be up there in the sky, with all your make-up on and your hair all pretty and that lovely big *smile* on your face!
	See that, Judith? A lovely big smile on her face. And it's no even her birthday.
Jude	And their mothers would hover behind them like birds of prey, nails like talons, shrieking and descending if the girls got a wee splodge of jam on their dress.
	And I'd sit there in my 'party frock'.
	And I remember watching all of this, at the end of the table, all these beautiful little girls. In pink. Lilac. Lavender. Yellow. And I looked at my glass of Coke. How black it was. And without even knowing why I was doing it, my hand just lifted the glass and…
Mum	Judith! Judith, what are you *doing*? Oh yer dress, Judith. Yer dress, it's ruined. C'mere. Oh madam, I just hope you didn't do that on purpose!

Jude	My first…protest.
	I was *six*.
Adam	Didn't like wearin pretty things, oor Judy. Kinday queer that way.
Maryann	Kinday what?
Jude	Didn't see why I should have to.
Adam	(*laughs*) Why ye talkin like that, Judy?
Jude	Like what?
Adam	'Didn't see why I should have to.'
Jude	Didn't…see…why… I'm not sure what you're getting at, Adam.
Adam	Ye're still daein it.
Jude	I am not.
Adam	Ye're *still* daein it.
Jude	Still daein fuckin whit!

Adam smiles.

Jude	(*harrassed*). Let's just look at the menu, shall we?
Maryann	By the way, the Vietnamese ca'song salmon is beautiful in here.
Jude	Might just have the salad.

Maryann	Still on your diet, sweetie?
Adam	It's sweeties that's the problem!
Jude	Yeah. Three pounds this week.
Maryann	That's my girl.
Jude	What are you having, Adam?
Adam	Macaroni and chips.
Jude	You always have macaroni.
Adam	I likes macaroni.
Jude	What about the braised scallops? You'd like scallops.
Adam	Barf-o-rama! What's a scallop?
Maryann	It's a kind of seafood.
Adam	Well that's me. I see food and eat it! So macaroni and chips it is.
Judy	I don't think they do macaroni.
Adam	Ye whit? Kinda place is this!
Maryann	One of the best in Glasgow.
Adam	Cannay be that good, doesnay do macaroni!
Jude	Adam, please. You can get macaroni anywhere.
Adam	That's whit I mean!

Judy	Don't show me up. Not today.
Maryann	That's okay, Judith. Adam, have what you want.
Adam	I want macaroni!
Waiter	Can I take your drinks order?
Jude	Yes. I think we're going to have the wine. Perhaps a Sauvignon Blanc? Or a Chardonnay...?
Maryann	Let's have Pinot. I'm in a Pinot mood.
Jude	Pinot.
Waiter	And you, sir?
Adam	Irn-Bru.
Waiter	I'm afraid we don't do Irn-Bru, sir.
Adam	Irn-Bru please.
Jude	They don't do Irn-Bru, Adam.
Adam	I'll just have an Irn-Bru then.
Jude	Coke for him.
Waiter	No problem. I'll be back in a moment for your food order.
Adam	Poofy bastard.
Maryann	Sorry?

Adam	Nae Irn-Bru! Can ye believe that?
Maryann	What did he just say?
Adam	He said there's nae Irn-Bru.
Maryann	'Poofy?'
Adam	Aye, I thought so tae. See the way he walks?
Jude	Listen. You can't just.
Maryann	C'mon, Adam, that's not really on.
Adam	Darn tootin! Nae Irn-Bru?
Jude	Maryann, I did explain this to you.
Adam	Better have macaroni, I'm warnin yese…
Maryann	(*sighs*) Okay okay okay okay.
Adam	Don't make me angry.
Jude	He doesn't. He can't.
Adam	You won't like me when I'm angry.

Doom.

Doom.

Doom.

Jude	Presents! Um, why don't you both give me your presents?

Maryann   Yes, why not.

Jude   Been waiting all week for this.

Adam   Goody, Judy!

Maryann passes Jude her gift.

Maryann   It's nothing much, I just.

Jude tears it open.

Adam   Ooh, excitin! Hurry up, Jude! Is it a squid?

Jude   It's a…book.

Adam   A comic book?

Jude   'With the striking logic that is his trademark, Chomsky dissects America's quest for global supremacy, tracking the US government's aggressive pursuit of policies intended to achieve full-spectrum dominance at any cost.'

Adam   Yawnsville Arizona, dudes.

Maryann   Some light reading for you.

Jude   Brilliant, Maryann, thanks.

Adam   Me turn!

Jude unwraps Adam's gift.

Jude   Queen's Greatest Hits?

Adam	Best band there's ever been!
Maryann	I didn't know you liked Queen.
Jude	Neither did I. Uh, thanks, Adam. I can see you put a lot of thought into that one.
Adam	Hey. It's a kinda magic.
Maryann	Oh, I got you something else.
Jude	Really? You spoil me, Maryann. What's this? It's soft. Clothing.
Adam	Whit if it's a dress, dudes? Hide the Cola!
Jude	It's. Underwear.
Maryann	You like?
Jude	Um. Maryann. Not in front of. Um.
Adam	You runnin out of underwear, Jude? Cos I nearly got ye socks.
Maryann	Oh. I thought you'd like it…
Jude	I do. It's just that. He can't. He doesn't.
	Och, I'm sorry, Maryann. Don't listen to me. It's beautiful, thank you.

They kiss. Adam watches this.

Doom.

Doom.

Doom.

Adam   Look at the lights, dudes.

Maryann and Jude freeze in the kiss.

The lights.

Gold.

Above their heads.

Happycoloured.

He looks at his hands. Crackle, fizz.

This one time I got mice for ma birthday.
Always wantin mice.

Mam, can I get mice?

Mother   Ye'll no take care of them, Adam, I ken ye'll no.

Adam   I will. Every day. I promise. I'll feed them and change
their straw and their water and love them, Mam. I will.
I'll tooooootally love them.

Mother   Aye, alright. But you're responsible for them, Adam. I'm
no wantin them gettin oot and roamin aw over the hoose.

Adam   Duh! Zif!

So I got them mice and dudes they were so annoyin. Ye're tryin tae get tae sleep at nights and aw ye can hear is them on that wheel.

Drrrdt drrrrdt drrrrdt drrrrdt.

Never stopped wi that wheel!

Drrrdt drrrrdt drrrrrdt drrrrdt. Drrrrdt drrrrrdt. Drrrrrdt drrrrrdt. Aw day!

So I just let them oot.

Dad said

Ye did whit?

I let them oot, Dad.

Noo they're gonnay be all over the place! They'll breed! There'll be dozens of them before ye ken it.

I'm sorry, Dad.

Ye're sorry? Ye're always sorry. Ya stupit dense bloody-

I ken, Dad.

I ken.

I'm stupit.

I'm dense.

Then I heard them, dudes…

Squeak squeak. Why did ye let us go, Sparkeeee? Why didn't ye love us, Sparkeeee. Squeak. Just wanted you to love us, Sparkeeee.

Why didn't I love yese? Cose yese are stupit. Cos yese are wee and pointless and stupit. Get it?

Found one. Behind the couch. Stoatin aboot.

Oh, hello wee man. Are ye scared? Aw, I'm sorry, pal. C'mere. That's it, wee man. Come tae Sparky. I'm sorry. Come on....

He stamps on it.

Fuck ye.

American   All over the world people know what they want when they eat here. They want speedy service, they want friendly service, they want the good wholesome food that we're happy to provide. So you're thinking: how do we achieve this? Two words. Team work. If a crew-member fails in his or her duties then it affects all of us. It won't work no other way. That's why we are number one in the fast food market. That's why people love to dine here. That's why we are WINNERS.

Music: 'Flash' by Queen. Adam standing outside McDonalds in costume, handing out flyers.

Adam   Come in and eat, dudes. Our burgers are herolicious! Sir?

Madam? The burger that stops burglars!

Passer-by   Who you meantay be?

Adam   I'm The Incredible Adam Spark, sir.

Passer-by   And what are ye standin here for?

Adam   I'm here to save the world, sir. And persuade you to try our new Hero Sandwich. Kryptonite with every bite!

Passser-by   I'm fine, thanks.

Angie   Bright spark?

Doom. Doom. Doom.

Adam   Doctor Doom? Thought he was defeated at the end of the last film, dudes!

Angie   I had you inside cleanin the toilets, Adam. Whit the hell ye doin out here?

Adam   My name's not Adam, maam.

Angie   Why ye talkin in that ridiculous American accent?

Adam   What American accent, maam?

Angie   That one! And is that a leotard?

Adam   Aye alright, Angie, it's me. But listen, I'm only tryin tae promote our new burger, ken? Showin injun-yoo-ity Thought it might get me employee of the month?

Angie   Bright Spark. Listen. First of all, ye're no doin what I telt ye to do. Looks like the Roman Army passed thru them toilets, every one of them needin a shite. Secondly, ye have to get permission to pull a stunt like this. And I'd have to get permission from the Regional Manager. Who'd need permission from Marketing at Head Office. Which'd probably be denied.

Adam   How?

Angie   I'll tell ye how, bright spark. Cos this company's vision is NOT to be interfered with.

Adam   But the injun-yoo-ity…?

Angie   That's no how it works, sonny. All over the world we give customers exactly the same in every single city. Exactly. The. Same. Package it, market it, sell it. Enday story. From New York to Tokyo. That's why this is one of the biggest companies in the world, bright spark. No cos of superpowers and leotards.

Adam   Aye? Whit if Flash Gordon approached ye for a job then?

Angie   Whit dae ye mean Flash Gordon approaching?

Adam   Open fire! All weapons!

Dispatch war rocket Ajax! To bring back his body!

Heh heh heh.

Angie stands with her arms folded.

Adam   Queen!

Angie stands with her arms folded.

Adam   Aye, so what was it ye wanted?

Angie   Listen. We've got a new start the day, want ye tae take her round, show her the ropes. She's kinda, em, on your wavelength. If ye ken whit I mean.

Bright spark, this is Bonnie.

Bonnie   Hiya, bright spark.

Adam   Hiya, Bonnie.

Angie   Take her inside and show her howtay cook the burgers. And nae mair Queen or superheroes.

They head indoors.

Bonnie   So you like Queen?

Adam   And superheroes! In fact, I sometimes imagines whit superheroes Queen would be if they were superheroes. Freddie would be Superman, cos he's super, man. Brian May would be

Bonnie   Mr Fantastic.

Adam   Cos he's

Bonnie   Fantastic.

Adam   Aye! And Roger Taylor would be

Bonnie   Han Solo.

Adam   Drum solo!

Bonnie   He's taylor made for it!

Adam   And that other one would be…?

They think. Shrug.

Together Another one.

Bonnie   I like yer costume, by the way.

Adam   Betty Ross, Lois Lane, Mary-Jane. She's byoootiful, dudes!

              Ooh thanks.

Adam works on flipping burgers while they talk.

Bonnie   Is that your nickname? Bright spark?

Adam   I prefer Sparky.

Bonnie   Like an electric shock?

Adam   Zactly.

Bonnie   Dzzt!

Adam   Ha ha. Do you have any nicknames?

Bonnie   Well. Um. No really. At school they used to call me Snotpants.

Adam   Have ye got snot in your pants?

Bonnie   They usedtay think so. Sometimes they'd…check.

Adam   I used to get dickbreath quite a lot.

Bonnie   That's just stupid.

Adam   I ken, cos-

Bonnie   -how can ye have breath like a dick?

Adam   Totally!

Bonnie   Dicks don't have breath.

Adam   Pants don't have snot.

Bonnie   Whit other ones did ye get?

Adam   Em, let me see. Fannybaws. Monkeybaws. Muppet.

Bonnie   Muppet?

Adam   Must've got tired of things with baws.

Bonnie   Whit's wrong with muppetbaws?

Adam   Mibbe muppets don't have baws.

Bonnie   But neither do fannys.

Adam   *(shrug)*

Bonnie   I got knobtart.

Adam	Knobtart? Whit's a knobtart?
Bonnie	(*shrug*) A tart who likes knobs?
Adam	Do you like knobs?
Bonnie	No really.
Adam	Well then. People who talk like that are just spastics.
Bonnie	Thickos.
Adam	Mongols!
Bonnie	Retards!
Adam	Lesbians!
Bonnie	Lesbians?
Adam	Totally!
Bonnie	Em. Ever get yer head flushed down the lav?
Adam	All the time, dude! Here we go again. Flssssssh gurgle gurgle. You?
Bonnie	Aye. The big girls used to do it tae me. Usedtay hide from them in the toilets.
Adam	Well that's just daft. That's where they were gonnay take ye anyway.
Bonnie	Oh aye. Shoulda thought of that.

Adam   *Psst.* Bit thick this yin, dudes.

Bonnie   Sparky?

Adam   Yo!

Bonnie   Why ye dressed like a superhero anyway?

Adam   Well, Bonnie, it's like this. I can like slow time down and speed it up and see lights round folk's heids that kinday tells me what kinday mood they're in and I had this accident at the gala day right and I totally saved this wean who like ran intay the middle of the Merican fitba then I woke up so now I'm thinkin mibbe this means I've been sent tae become like Falkirk's first superhero? and that I'm meantay save the world? So I thought I'd start by just...em...givin out flyers.

Bonnie   (*pause*)

                  Cool.

                  So ye can see lights round folk's heids?

Adam   Sure *thang.*

Bonnie   Whit light's round ma heid?

Adam   Gold.

Bonnie   And whit does that mean?

Adam   It means ye're happy.

Bonnie and Adam look at each other.

Bonnie   So.

Adam   So.

Bonnie   Ye gonnay show me
The

Rope...

...s?

A burst of flames. The burger-grill starts beeping. Adam backs away from it, clutching his arm.

Angie   Bright spark! Ye didn't see that the burgers were on fire?

Adam   Um.

Angie   Away in a dream world the two of yese! Ya stupit bloody. Oh, I can see how this is gonnay turn oot. *Made* for each other, you pair.

Bonnie   Hear that?

Adam   Made for each other.

She touches his arm.

Bonnie   Were ye burnt?

Adam   Burnt? Ach, superheroes don't feel pain. Unless it's. Ken. Cos of Judy.

Bonnie   Who's Judy?

Adam   She used to be ma sister. Before she wentay uni.

Bonnie   I don't get it. How can somebody *used* to be yer sister?

Adam   Well. Ken. Just like Mam and Dad used to be Mam and Dad.

Bonnie   How? Whit happened tae them? Did they got to uni tae?

Adam   Naw.

Sounds of a gale.

Mam   Paper is it? Pub is it? Fitba is it? Ye ken I havetay cope with this wean all week. Whit dae ye mean Saturday's your day? Cos ye work? Cos ye *work?* Ye think this wean's no work? Ye think this wean's no WORK?

Adam   I'm work.

Mam   Aye well, ken whit? On ye go then! On ye go and don't come back, ya bloody…

The wind picks up. Mam takes stuff out of the wardrobe and throws it into the street.

Then she goes round the room smashing furniture, screaming.

Adam watches this, mute.

Mam stands weeping, surveys the wreckage of the room. She sees Adam outside witnessing this. She crosses to him and they embrace. Then she walks back into the house.

Sits down.

Removes pills from a bottle.

And swallows them.

Pill after pill.

The storm is raging.

We see her gradually falling unconscious. Wind roars. The house begins to spin, faster and faster. It lifts off into the air! Bonnie and Adam watch it go.

Adam   Somewhere over the rainbow, way up high....

There's a land that I heard of, once in a lullaby...

Bonnie   So she never came back?

Adam   Naw. She's still there. Still tryin tae find her way hame probably. I have to get there and help her, Bonnie. She'll no manage it herself.

Bonnie   Aye, of course. But whit aboot yer sister? Judy? She in Oz tae?

Adam   Naw. She's in Glesga.

Bonnie   Glesga. Who with?

Adam   (*grumbles*) The Wicked Witch of the West.

Bonnie   Who?

Adam   Never mind.

Bonnie   Well why don't ye just go to Oz and find your Mam?

Adam   Tornadoes don't just come along every day likes.

Bonnie   We could walk there.
Adam   Don't ken the way!

Munchkins   Ding-dong the witch is dead...

Bonnie   Well I'm finished ma shift. We could just start walkin and
            see if we find her.

Adam   Which old witch?

Munchkins   The wicked witch

Bonnie   Aye. Take ma hand, Adam.

            See.

            How does that feel?

Adam   Em. Aye, Bonnie. Feels alright.

Bonnie   Good.

Adam   Pals.

Bonnie   Pals.

Munchkins   Ding-dong the wicked witch is dead!

Adam   We just follow the yellow brick road?

Bonnie   And see where it leads. It'll be an adventure.

Adam   I like adventures.

Bonnie   Me too.

Adam   I like you, Bonnie.

Bonnie   I like you, Adam.

Munchkins   Behold! Behold behold!

Adam   I'm havin fun. Let's march.

Bonnie   'kay.

They start marching, grinning.

Adam   Ding-dong the witch is dead!

Bonnie   Which old witch?

Adam   The wicked witch.

Crowd   No war!

Bonnie/Adam   Ding-dong the wicked witch is dead.

Jude and Maryann enter, leading a protest march.

Crowd   No war!

Bonnie/Adam   Which old witch? The wicked witch!

Crowd   No war!

Jude and Maryann march alongside Adam and Bonnie, link arms with Adam. Bonnie is swept away from Adam in the crowd.

Adam	Bonnie?
Judy	C'mon, Adam, say it: No War!
Maryann	No War!
Judy	Say: No War!
Maryann	No War!
Adam	Bonnie?

She is gone, out of reach.

Judy	I'm so glad you decided to come, Adam. It's important that we take a stand against these criminals.
Adam	Listen, Jude. Somethin to tell ye.
Judy	What's that, Adam?
Crowd	No War!
Adam	I've met somebody. This girl. From work.
Crowd	No War!
Judy	What? You'll have to shout!
Adam	I said I've met this girl at my work! She's really nice. Tooooootally like her. She's better than you!
Judy	What? You've met a girl? That's *great*, Adam. I'm so pleased for you.

Judy   Hear that, Maryann? Adam's got a girlfriend.

Maryann   Really? Fantastic, Adam!

Maryann tries to hug him but his look stops her.

Adam   So whit's this march for, Judy?

Judy   Well, Adam, it's quite difficult to explain.

How can I describe it…

See if there's one thing I hate, it's a bully.

Whether it's them Animalz on the scheme.

Or it's America.

Or it's Ad- I mean, Dad.

Adam   It's who?

Judy   Dad.

Adam   You said 'Ad-'

Judy   No I didn't.

Adam   'No I didn't.'

Naw.

Ye.

Didnay.

| | Aye. Anyway. The war. Whose side we on? |
| **Maryann** | Well, *I'm* not on anybody's *side*, as such, Adam. |

Coloured lights round Maryann's head.

Adam   Sure about that, Maryann? Cos the lights are tellin a different story.

Judy   But George W. Bush, Adam. He's a bully.

Maryann   And Saddam Hussein, Adam. He's a bully too.

Judy   So what do ye do with bullies?

Adam   (*staring at Maryann*) Kill them.

Jude   You don't kill them, Adam, no. But you have to stand up to them. Reason with them.

H-Glen Animlaz run onstage, grab Adam, flush his head down the toilet. Then they run off in the other direction, laughing.

Maryann   No War!

Judy   No War! C'mon, Adam! No?

Adam   War!

Judy   No?

Adam   War!

Judy   No?

Adam   War!

Judy   No?

Adam   War!

War!

War!

War!

WAR!

WAR!

Stage goes red.

The lights.

The lights, dudes.

Like

Blood.

A whole big flood.

Rainin.

Rainin down.

On the streets.

And the rivers.

And the peeps.

And the weans.

Red red rain.

Come down.

Come down.

Adam closes his eyes, stands, grinning, bathing in it.

Socialist   This war is not about weapons of mass destruction.

Adam   Dee-struck-shin…

Socialist   Or about bringing democracy to the Middle East. It is about power.

Adam   Power…

Socialist   We will reject this war!

Adam   War…

Socialist   We will reject this capitalist system of evil…

Adam   Evil…

Socialist   Because what this has shown, yet again, is that Scotland is being ruled by an alien government.

Adam's eyes spring open. Crowd roars. Whistles.

Adam   Alien guvvirment?

Alien guvvirment, dudes!

We're being ruled by...*aliens?*

Holy martians, Batman, I've gottay tell Judy!

Adam frantically searches for her through the crowd.

Judy?

Judy!

We're being ruled by an alien guvvirment!

Martians, Judy!

The Martians have landed!

Judy...?

Where are ye...?

He's scared now, swamped by the crowd.

Judy! Judy! Where are y...

Sees Jude and Maryann kissing.

Judy...?

Passionately.

Judy.

Crowd noise drops away.
Everything is still.

Silent.

Red.

Adam stands and watches them.

Breathing.

Uncomprehending.

Then things speed back up – horrifically. The crowd noise is deafening. Adam roars and lunges at Maryann.

Crowd   Ding-dong the witch is dead!

He hauls her off of Judy, punches her. Throws her to the ground. We can't hear his words but he is seething and spitting.

Crowd   Ding-dong the wicked witch is dead!

Jude is screaming, trying to pull them apart. Adam starts kicking Maryann. She curls into a ball. Then he lands on her, punches her in the face. Over and over and over and

Black.

Adam   Dad?

            Adam…

            Whit is it, Dad?
            Look up there, Adam. At the sky. At the stars.

Whoah!

Look at them!

Me and Dad, right, we usedtay go fishin. Loch Ness, Loch Shin, Loch Awe. Loch Aye the Noo!

Night time.

Quiet.

Shh.

Water goin lap lap lap.

Dad's big arms round me mmmmmmmm showin me howtay cast.

Splsh!

Reeeeeeel.

Look up, Adam. Look at the stars.

Brrrrrrrrrrp millions of them!

But it's no the stars, dudes, it's that big space between them.

Black

Black

Dad?

Aye, son?

How come you and Mum shout at each other?

>   (*pause*)

>   Well, Adam, sometimes Mummys and Daddys they
>   don't always agree. And sometimes when they disagree
>   strongly. They get angry with each other.

Have ye ever…hit her?

>   Whit d'ye mean, Adam?

>   Did she tell ye that?

>   That I've hit her?

Naw.

Judy did.

>   Oh did she?

>   Oh did she now?

Judy doesn't lie, Dad.

Says ye hit oor Mam.

>   Well.

>   Men can be.

>   Weak.

And

Ashamed.

Weak?

When Mike Tyson Lennox Lewis Muhammed Ali they hitcha with a left hook – ba-doof! They don't look weak to me, dudes.

Aye, well.

Weakness it is, son.

It's nothin tae be prouday.

But I promise ye. I'll never dae it again.

Never?

Never.

Ye'd never hit me, Dad, would ye?

Naw, son.

You're ma boy.

You're

ma

boy.

That's whit I thought, Dad.

I'm yer boy.

Mmmmm.

I'm sayin

Dad

I'm yer boy, aren't I?

Dad?

Da-aad?

Ye there?

Dad…

Brrrr.

It's cold, Dad.

Come back.

It's dark

Dad?

The bell rings for the Witching Hour. Skeletons start to dance onstage.

No. Stop.

Demons.

Whit dae ye want wi me?

Horror movie monsters.

> I didn't mean to to do it! I didn't mean to hurt her!

They form a snaking line, twisting sinuously towards him, cackling and clawing. Adam tries to run from them, but others appear from the shadows to block his path. The drums from the protest march sound:

Doom.

Doom.

Doom.

> I was weak.

> That was all.

> Tell them, Dad.

> Get them away from me, Dad.

> Dad!

> Mam!

Their claws reach for him.

> Judy!

> Anybody!

They close in, moaning, almost touching his face.

> I didn't meantay hurt her.

No!

     Noooooooo

Lights change.

Animalz Trick or treat?

Adam   Eh?

Animalz C'mon then, Sparky.

     Get yer money oot.

     For the guisers.

     Trick or treat!

     Smell ma feet!

     Give us somethin nice to eat!

Adam   Em. Aye guys. I thought.

Animalz Aw, ye weren't scared, were ye?

     Look at this, boys.

     Feart!

     Just costumes, Sparky.

     No mindin whit night it is?
     Halloween.

Moo ha ha ha!

Look at this yin.

Who am I, Sparky?

Adam   Em. Wolverine.

Animalz   Wolverine? I'm Freddy Krueger, ya bawbag!

I'm Jason.

Pinheid.

Mair like dickheid.

Or pin-dick!

Well c'mon then, Sparky.

Adam   Whit?

Animalz   Geez some money.

Halloween.

For the guisers and that.

Adam fishes in his pocket for some change. Gives it to the Animalz. They look at it. They look at him. He goes into his pocket again. Brings out a note this time.

Animalz   That's better.
Lottay effort went intay these costumes.

Ya tight-fisted wee.

Hey. *You* can talk.

They call this yin Merlin.

Disappears when it's his round.

*Any*way, Sparky.

Where's yer costume?

Adam   Oh.

Always bring it with me. Just in case there's any crime needs fought on the mean streets of Falkirk.

Dresses in mask. Cape.

Animalz   Look at this.

The Incredible Adam Spark eh?

Is it a bird?

Is it a plane?

Naw, it's just a *dick*.

So!

Fought any crime yet, Sparky?

Adam   Aye.

In Glesga likes. On this protest march. Gave oot a right leatherin. Just flew right in there. Whoof! Smack! Ba-doof. They went doon, hit the deck. Blegh.

Animalz   That right?

Protest march?

Wis it the cops?

Ye fight the riot police!

Whoof!

Adam   Naw. Somebody's who's been messin aboot wi ma sister.

Animalz   Yer sister?

But.

Thought she was a-

Wheesht youse.

Ignoramuses.

We wantay hear this story.

Aye.

So.

Yer sister.

Gottay stick up for the faimly.

Somebody messin yer sister aboot?

Cardinal sin.

Whit happened, Sparky?

On ye go.

Adam   So. Got her doon on the ground, and I'm like that – Doof doof doof.

Animalz   Her?

Adam   Aye.

Animalz   Yer sister?

Adam   Her girlfriend.

Animalz   It was her girlfriend ye leathered?

Adam   Em.

Animalz   A woman?

Adam   Aye.

Animalz stare at each other.

Animalz   Kinday animal are you?

Adam   But boys…

Animals   But boys nothin.

Ye dinnae hit women, Sparky.

That's shockin.

Whoah.

This yin's wild.

Mental.

Crazy.

Adam   I'm no mental.

Animalz   Ootay control.

Psycho.

Heidcase.

Adam   I'm no a heidcase.

Animalz   Brutal

Nutjob.

Wido.

Paedo.

Adam   Stop callin me that. Look boys, I was walkin that wee lassie hame yon time. She was lost. I was helpin her.

The Animalz start to shrink back into the darkness.

She couldnay find her way and I was helpin her. That's aw.

That's aw.

Animalz disappear into the night. Sound of phone ringing.

Jude   "Sorry, Adam and I aren't here to take your call right now. Probably pottering around somewhere. Please leave a message and I'll get back to you as soon as I can."

Adam   "Or I'll get back to you."

Jude   "One of us will get back to you."

Adam   (*pause*) "Probably her"

Beep!

Maryann   Hi, Judith. If you're there, pick up. Nope? God I hate talking to these things. Ok, well, I just wanted to say that uh I called the estate agent and they said that for this area of Glasgow it really is cheap. So I think we should get an offer in pretty soon. And that's all there is left to do really.

Except tell

You

Know

Who.

Okay, sweetheart, call me tomorrow. Hope everything's okay there. I love you. Be strong, Judith. You need to do this.

Dial tone.

Red light across the stage. Adam's hands are flaming. The dial tone rises in volume till it's an ugly drone. The Animalz, in their skeleton and demon costumes, make eerie sounds. Adam roars and flies off at top speed, wind screaming past his face.

Lands.

Hands clenched.

Birds tweeting, sound of rushing water.

Adam   Bonnie?

Bonnie   Sparky.

                You're still in costume.

Adam   Aye, em. Just finished work likes.

Bonnie   Give out many leaflets today?

Adam   Yup, Bonnie, sure did. Man's gottay do what a man's gottay do. And sometimes that involves LEAFLETING!

Bonnie   It's a good promotion, the Hero Sandwich. You're doin really well. The kids love it.

Adam   Well, I loves the kids! So all's fair.

Bonnie   Wanna come walk with me? Along the canal?

Adam   Where does it go?

Bonnie	The Falkirk Wheel. Ye been before?
Adam	Naw, but I've heard it's Wheely good!
Bonnie	Ha ha.
Adam	Let's go, dude!

They start walking. Bonnie looks at him, takes his hand.

Bonnie	Everything alright, Sparky?
Adam	Aye. Course. Why would it no be?
Bonnie	Ye look tense.
Adam	Aye. I've got tennis elbow.
Bonnie	Oh here, did I tell ye? Me and Mum and Dad and my two wee brothers, we went to the Mariner Centre in Camelon and went swimmin, then we all went out to the Coppertop and had lunch. I had like a big giant knickerbocker glory. Total *that* size.
Adam	Ha ha. Knickers! Ha ha. Bockers!
Bonnie	Whit did you dae last night?
Adam	Nothin. Stayed in. Watched telly.
Bonnie	With Jude?
Adam	Jude was in Glesga.
Bonnie	She's *always* in Glesga.

Adam   Tell me aboot it. She's bought a flat with Maryann.

Bonnie   That's great.

Adam   Aye.

Bonnie   You gonnay go live with them?

Adam   Nah, too much hassle, Bonnie. Ma job's through here. Bein a hero. Servin the weans of Falkirk. Servin... burgers.

Bonnie   Good.

Adam   Whit's good?

Bonnie   That ye're stayin here.

Adam   How?

Bonnie   Take off yer mask. Let me see yer eyes.

Bonnie takes off his mask. His cape. It drops to the floor. He looks away, but she pulls his face back to hers.

Bonnie   Whit's wrong, Sparky?

Adam   I've done things.

Bonnie   Whit? Whit've ye done?

Adam   Nothin. It's. I'm not.

              Bonnie?

I'm not one of the...

Baddies..?

Am I?

Bonnie   Naw, Sparky. Naw. Ye're not a baddie.

Bonnie kisses him. Adam's eyes are wide open. He doesn't know what to do with his hands. He places them on Bonnie's waist. Then her shoulders. Then her waist.

Bonnie   Did ye like that?

Adam   Does the Pope shit in the woods?

Bonnie puts her face on his shoulder, smiles. Carefully he places his arms around her, till it feels natural. He starts to relax, letting her cuddle into him. He touches her hair.

Bonnie   Oh, Adam. That feels nice.

Adam   First time she's called me Adam, dudes.

The very first time.

Bonnie   I like the way ye hold me, Adam.

Adam   I like holdin ye, Bonnie.

Man comes past with a dog, which starts sniffing about them.

Adam tuts.

Bonnie starts to pet the dog.

Dog-walker   Sorry about this. Right you, c'mon now. That's enough.

Bonnie   Oh it's fine, I love Alsations.

Dog-walker   Obedient dogs.

Bonnie   They are. So loyal. And he's beautiful. Look at his gorgeous big coat, Adam.

Adam   Aye. Smart.

Bonnie   Aw, he's wuvvawy boy. Aren't you? Aren't you a wuvvawy boy?

Stage freezes. Red light.

Dog   Jealous?

Adam   Whit, dude? Jealous of a dog. Zif!

Dog   I think you're jealous.

Adam   You. Sniff. Bums.

Dog   Why do you deny your true nature, Adam Spark?

Adam   Oh aye, this'll be good. Comin from an Alsation? A foreigner! Whit's my true nature, likes?

Dog   Your animal nature.

To hurt.

To kill.

Adam   Oh aye, and how would *you* ken?

Dog   I share this nature.

I have been civilised by my master. I have grown accustomed to the hands of humans upon me. Women. Children. I let them pet my coat and stroke my ears. I roll over and allow them to tickle my belly. I let them patronise me, to feel superior.

Yes, my master. No, my master. I am your humble servant, my master.

But.

I have a sense of smell which I use to hunt prey.

I have canine teeth, which tear and rend.

I eat *meat*.

Adam   Who are you?

Dog   I am of the great Alsation race. The Nazis used us to sniff out the Jews. Other…empires…have found our ferocity helpful in dealing with their enemies.

Have you ever seen a naked man blindfolded, Adam Spark?

Cowering?
Do you understand that kind of power?

We are no lap dogs.

For should any human ever be so bold as to test us…

Leaps forward at Adam, snarling.

Dog-walker   Hey you! That's enough. That's enough!

Adam   Whoah.

Dog-walker   I'm sorry. He's not usually this way. Come on!

Bonnie   I don't think he likes you, Adam.

Dog-walker   Better get him out of here. Right you! That's enough.

Bonnie   Where did that come from?

Adam   That's why I don't like animals, Bonnie. They can turn.

Bonnie   He must've picked up on somethin. Ken how they have a sixth sense? They can smell a threat.

Adam   But I'm no a threat. Keep tryin to *tell* people this, dude.

  I was takin that wee lassie hame that time. I was takin her *hame*. Not away, like they all thought.

Bonnie   Whit ye talkin about?

Adam   I don't. Like. *Dogs*. Don't like the things they *say*.

Bonnie   Mibbe it's your superpowers. Mibbe he could sense that you're, ken, different.

Adam   Different? Aye. Different.

Bonnie	Adam, ye're shakin. You poor thing. Did he scare ye? It's ok. Sorry, I shouldn't have started pettin him. I didn't ken ye don't like dogs. C'mere.

She embraces him again. When she tries to pull away he pulls her back in.

Adam	Don't let me go, Bonnie.
Bonnie	Adam…
Adam	I don't ken what'll happen if ye do.
Bonnie	I have to let go sometime.
Adam	No ye don't.
Bonnie	Ok. Ok, I won't.

They continue the embrace.

Adam	I like that you're different too, Bonnie.
Bonnie	I'm not different, Adam.
	I'm the same.
Adam	Aye.
	We're the same.

They kiss again, more urgently this time. Their hands start to roam. They sink towards the ground. Birds singing. He bites her neck. She gasps. He starts to growl.

Bonnie	Yes, Adam.

That feels good.

Oh yes, Adam.

Right there…

Just there…

Bite me.

The dog reappears at the side of the stage, watching.

Fade.

Lights up on a restaurant, where Jude and Maryann sit. Adam observes them from the corner of the room.

Judy   He'll be here.

Maryann   I don't want him to be here.

Judy   Well, I think it's for the best if he comes. It'll be a good sign.

Maryann   We'll see.

But if he lays one finger on me, that's it, Judith. I will not have that *thing* in my life.

Judy   Hey. Don't call him a *thing*. He's my brother.

Maryann   Yes he is, Judith. Yes he is. And he's always going to be your brother, isn't he? He's always going to be there.

Judy   I won't have him at the flat, okay? I'll visit him in Falkirk. You don't have to see him if you don't want to.

Maryann   But you do.

Judy   Yes.

                I do.

Maryann   He's been allowed to act like a child all his life, Judith. It's no wonder he has tantrums. Except these tantrums come out of the body of a man. A full-grown man. Are you expecting him to be able to change now? I mean, he's only had a *year* to get used to this.

Judy   People can change.

Maryann   Did your father change?

Judy   (*pause*)

                He did actually.

Maryann   Yes. By leaving.

Judy looks at her watch, drums her fingers on the table.

Maryann   Still think he's going to come?

Judy   If he comes that means he's sorry.

Maryann   And if he doesn't?

Judy   That means he's scared.

Maryann   Ah, I see.

         He's the scared one.

         Ok.

Mayrann stands, puts her jacket on.

Judy   Where are you going? I told you. He'll come. Give him
         time..

Maryann   Look, I'll see you at the library on Monday. You've got
         exams next week, you can't afford this kind of stress.

         Just like you can't afford this kind of flat.

Judy   What do you mean? Course I can afford it. I've got
         Mum's life insurance and once I've graduated and I'm
         earning-

Maryann   That's not what I meant, Judith.

Maryann exits.

Judy   He'll come, Maryann!
         He'll come around!

Judy folds her napkin, drinks from her wine. Places her face into her hands.
Adam addresses the audience.

Adam   Ka-pow! The Incredible Adam Spark, having saved the town from the giant squid – its squillions of squiddy tenty-kles – must become mild-mannered Sparky again. No-one can know his secret nature. Least of all, his sister, Judith. Does she suspect? Has she found his costyoom at the back of the wardrobe, the key to his true identity? Stay tuned, dudes…

Comes running up to Judy's table.

Adam Judy, so sorry, it was the-

Hey.

Have you lost weight?

Judy Aye.

Adam Good for you. Ye needed to.

Judy Thanks.

Adam Anyway, the train, Judy! Got on the wrong train, ended up in Edinburgh instead of Glesga. Totally different drexions! Dude, I mean Jude – how am I supposed to know what way's the Good Witch of the East and what way's the Wicked Witch of the West?

Looks round.

So where is she?

Judy stands and puts her jacket on.

Judy She got tired of waitin for you, Adam. I ken how she feels.

Adam   But, Judy.

Where ye goin?

I'm here tae say sorry.

To you and Maryann.

Jude   Too late, Adam.

Before Judy exits, Adam freezes her. He circles her, directing his rage at her.

Adam   Aye, but that's cosay the trains, Judy, like I telt ye.

It's never too late.

I can control time!

I can control *you!*

You will do exactly what I say, Judith Spark, understand?

Understand!

Oh jobbies.

Where am I now, dudes?

I mean.
It's no easy this, bein a hero.

Like Spider-Man says.

With great power.

Comes great responsibility.

So mibbe I just need tae *show* ye, Jude.

Show ye.

Whit.

Happens.

When…

(*pause*)

Or mibbe I should just let ye go.

Clicks his fingers. Jude unfreezes. Maryann opens her arms. Jude crosses the stage and walks into them.

Maryann   Did he come?

Judith shakes her head. Maryann takes her hand. They exit.

Adam alone onstage.

Carnival noises.

Announcer   Ladies and gents, welcome to the Hallglen Gala Day. The biggest day of the year. In Hallglen. See Falkirk Judo Club doing a display. Of Judo. See the Camelon Archers club. And no ladies, they won't give you free peach schnapps heh heh. We've got a pet show, ladies and gents. Cats! Fish! Catfish! Or come to the main stage and see Scotland's greatest Queen tribute band, Pure Dead Magic.

Bonnie cheers.

Adam   Bonnie, it's Queen!

Bonnie   Best band there's ever been!

Adam   Toooootally.

Bonnie   Don't ye wish Freddie Mercury was still alive?

Adam   He is. (*clutches heart*) In here.

Adam   He's the queen of hearts!

Bonnie   The heart of Queen!

Adam   It's a kinday magic.

She turns to face him. They stare at each other.

Bonnie   It is a kinday magic.

Adam   I really miss her, Bonnie.

Bonnie   Miss who?

Queen   Mamma

             Life had just begun…

             But now I've gone and thrown it all away.

Adam, Freddie and Bonnie sing together.

             Mamma….

Ooh ooh ooh ooooh.

Didn't mean to make you cry.

If I'm not back again this time tomorrow.

Carry on, carry on.

As if nothing really matters.

Song continues in background.

Animalz   Hey, Sparky.

Adam   Oh jobbies.

Bonnie   Whit is it?

Adam   Nothin. Just stick close tae me.

Hey, boys.

Animalz   Awright there, Sparky.

Gala Day eh!

No bad, no bad.

No as good as Big in Falkirk.

But then.

We're big in Falkirk.

Well. Some of us mair than others.

Heh heh.

Your mind's a midden.

Drink, Sparky?

They pass him a can of lager. He swigs, grimaces.

Adam   Cheers, boys. Tastes great.

Animalz   Who's the burd?

Adam   Oh. Eh. This is

Ma burd.

Bonnie.

Animalz   Pleased tae meet ye.

Bonnie?

No a wee bit old for you, Sparky?

Bonnie   Whit's that supposed tae mean?

Animalz   Aw, no telt her?
No telt her aboot the wean?

Bonnie   Whit's this aboot a wean, Sparky?

Animalz   His wee brush wi the law.

Cannae believe ye've no telt her.

Adam   Aye well. Been busy, boys.

Animalz   Been busy?

Busy daein whit?

Daein *who*?

This yin?

This *thing*?

Anyway.

We need ye the day, Sparky.

Got a *job* for ye.

Adam   Kinday job?

Animalz   Tammyhill Crew are here the day.

Actin smart.

Widos.

Think they run the place.

Turnin up here.

In Hallglen.

Askin for it.

Need Hallglen boys tae show them.

Tae show.

Nae.

Fear.

Adam   Well, em, I'd lovetay likes. But I'm kinday em. Busy the day, ken?

Animalz   Aye, we can see that.

Sorry, hen.

Needtay borrow yer man for a bit.

We'll get him backtay ye in one piece.

Mibbe two pieces.

Mon you.

Bonnie   Adam? Are you going with this lot?

Adam   Em. Sorry boys. Kinday like to spend the day wi ma girlfriend, ken?

Animalz   Naw.

We dinnae ken.

Ye don't understand, Sparky.

Whit d'ye think this is?

A youth club?

He wishes!

Think ye can just drop in and oot?

Hallglen boys.

We stick together.

Get it?

Now.

Move.

Bonnie   I think ye heard him, boys. He's no comin.

Animalz   Scuse me, hen?

Say somethin there?

They begin to circle her.

Bonnie   I said…

He's not.

Coming.

Animalz   That so?

Ye listenin tae this, Sparky.

A woman tellin ye whit tae dae?

Cannae have that.

We ken how ye feel aboot that, Sparky.

Women.

How ye deal with them, Sparky.

Gonnay tell her, Sparky?

Tell her the score.

Adam   Leave her alone.

His hands start flaming.

Animalz   Or whit?

You no take a tellin the last time?

When ye defended that Paki?

We telt ye whit would happen.

Had yer warnin.

They line up against him, begin to advance. Adam puts his mask and cape on. The song swells again.

Adam   Mamma!

Ooh ooh ooh oooh.

I don't wanna die.

Sometimes wish I'd never been born at all…

During the guitar solo he flies through the air. The Animalz chase him, snarling, try to grab him. He eludes them, blasting. Sometimes they grab Bonnie, but she escapes, terrified. This carries on until the opera section of the song, and…

They stand.

A fight takes place during the opera section of 'Bohemian Rhapsody', ends with Adam on the ground, being kicked repeatedly, Bonnie screaming.

Cut.

Silence.

Black.

Spotlight on Adam.

Blip

Blip

Blip

Adam wakes.

Adam   Hello?
       Hello?

       Is there anybody there?

       Whoah, dudes. I've a feelin we're not in Falkirk anymore.

Adam rises, walks the stage. Soon he arrives at a pair of giant, green gates. Looks up at them.

When he pushes them open, they make an ancient creaking sound.

He walks into the chamber.

Slowly.

Carefully.

Footsteps echoing.

Then flames erupt. Adam flinches. A giant, monstrous face appears.

Wizard   COME FORWARDS!

Adam   Dad? Is that you?

Wizard   I. AM. OZ. THE GREAT AND POWERFUL.

WHO ARE YOU?

Adam   I am Sparky. Eh. The small and stupit.

Wizard   WHAT DO YOU WANT?

Adam   Em. I wantay get back. Back to whit it was all like. Before. Me, Judy, Mam, you.

Wizard   THE GREAT AND POWERFUL OZ KNOWS WHY YOU HAVE COME.

Adam   ...well why did ye ask ...

Please, Dad. I did what you wanted. I always did everythin you wanted. I'm yer boy. Ye said it yerself. I'm yer-

Wizard   SILENCE!

Adam flinches again.

Adam   You outta be ashamed of yourself, Dad. Frightenin me like that when I came to you for help.

Wizard   I'LL HAVE TO GIVE THE MATTER A LITTLE THOUGHT. GO AWAY AND COME BACK TOMORROW.

Adam   Tomorrow? Always tomorrow, Dad. Ye're always busy. In the pub or at work or watchin the fitba. I need ye now.

Wizard   DO NOT AROUSE THE WRATH OF THE GREAT AND POWERFUL OZ. I SAID COME BACK TOMORROW!

Adam   If you were really great and powerful, ye'd keep yer promises.

To this family.

Wizard   HOW DARE YOU? DO YOU PRESUME TO CRITICISE THE GREAT OZ? YOU UNGRATEFUL CREATURE. THE GREAT OZ HAS SPOKEN.

Adam   No, Dad. I didn't mean-

Wizard   YOU LITTLE SHIT.

Adam   I'm sorry, Dad.

Wizard   MY PROMISES TO THIS FAMILY?

A SON LIKE YOU?

A WIFE LIKE HER?

A DYKE FOR A DAUGHTER?

Adam   No.

Wizard   C'MERE.

C'MERE, YA SPASTIC LITTLE BASTARD.

Adam   No, Dad.

Sounds of a fight. Smashing. Punching.

DON'T

YOU

EVER

DISOBEY

ME

AGAIN

Adam   (*sobbing, howling*) I just wantay go home. I just wantay go home!

Wizard   OH GOD. I'M SORRY, SON. I DIDN'T MEAN TO-

YOU JUST GOT IN THE WAY.

I'LL NEVER...

SON, PLEASE….

Adam   (*bawling*) Judy!

Wizard   PLEASE…

ADAM….

DON'T TELL YOUR MOTHER…

PLEASE…

Adam lies in the foetal position, sobbing. Shaking.

Enter Adam's Mother. She sees the pain he is in, covers her face with her hands, goes to him.

Mother   Oh, Adam. Oh my boy. What did he do to you?

Adam   It's alright, Mam. He didn't mean to scare me. He's just weak.

Mam   Shh, son.

Shh. I'm here.

I'm here now.

Blip

Blip

Blip

Light up on Judy, at the side of the hospital bed.

Adam   I did try, Mam.

Mam   I ken ye did, son. I saw ye.

Adam   They didnay make it easy for me, none of them. Ye understand that, don't ye?

Mam   Aye son. I understand. I understand ye.

Adam   I'm work.

Mam   Ye'll be no work here, Adam.

With me.

Adam   They don't want me back there, Mam. I'm different.

Mam   Well here everyone's different, son. Nobody minds.

Blip

Blip

Blip

Adam   I havetay go home, don't I, Mam?

I havetay fix it.

Mam   Aye, son.

Adam   But I don't wantay leave ye.

Can I come back here? Can I come back and visit ye one day?

Mam	We'll see. If ye're a good boy.
Adam	Yaay! I'll be a good boy. Wait and see, Mam.
	But how do I get hame?
Mam	You ken fine.
Adam	No, I don't.
Mam	Look.

Adam sees that he's wearing Judy's red shoes.

Adam	Judy's ruby slippers! Ooh they suit me, don't they?
Mam	All you have to do is click your heels together three times and say…
Adam	There's no place like home.
Mam	That's right.

Adam hugs her again. She kisses the top of his head.

Mam	Now remember, Adam. If ye don't behave yourself you won't be able to come back and see me.
Adam	I'll remember, Mam.
Mam	So be good.
Adam	I will.
Mam	Bye, son.

Adam   Bye, Mam.

Adam clicks his heels together three times, closes his eyes.

There's no place like home.

There's no place like home.

There's no place like home…

Mother takes her into her arms, carries him to the bed. Lays him down. Tucks him in. Kisses his head.

There's no place like home.

There's no place like home.

Mother fades.

Adam opens his eyes.

Blip.

Blip.

Judy   Adam?

Adam   Whoah.

Judy   Adam. You're awake!

Doctor!

Adam tries to sit up, winces with pain.

No, don't move, Adam.

Adam   No got much of a choice, Judy.

Doctor   Ah, there he is. You had us all worried for a while there, Adam. How do you feel?

Adam   Hm. Sure could do with a holiday to San Tropay, doctor. But other than that? I'm swell.

Whit happened, by the way? How did I get here?

Jude   It was them. Them animals. They gave ye a right going over at the Gala Day. Aw Adam, don't dae that to me! I thought I was gonnay lose you as well.

Doctor   You arrived here unconscious and this is the first time you've woken up since.

Adam   Like Dorothy in the poppy fields…

Jude   Whit's that?

Adam   Bonnie! Whit happened tae Bonnie, Jude?

Jude   She's fine, Adam. They didn't hurt her. Too busy hurtin you.

Adam   Just as well. Or I'd

(*winces*)

Ooh. Holy backpain, Batman!

Doctor   Now, just get plenty rest, Adam. It's going to take your body a while to get its strength back.

Adam   Strength...?

Looks at his hands. Tries to use them to speed time up. Nothing. Looks about the room.

No lights. Ma powers, dudes. They've...

Judy   Whit's up?

Adam   I'm not. I'm not a superhero anymore, Judy.

Judy   Oh, I wouldn't say that, Adam. Not accordin to the Falkirk Herald.

Adam   How dae ye mean?

Judy   (*reading*) "Hero Fights For His Life. A young man is in critical condition after surviving an attack from a vicious gang. Adam Spark, from Hallglen, is in intensive care in Falkirk Royal Infirmary, after defended his girlfriend, Bonnie Nisbet, during an assault. Five youths have been arrested and charged with grevious bodily harm."

Adam   Hero?

Judy   That's you, Adam.

Adam   I did the right thing?

Judy   Ye certainly did.

Enter Maryann

Maryann	Judith, I saw a doctor running here and I…
	Oh. Hello, Adam.
Adam	Hello, Maryann. Did you see the thing in the paper? I'm a hero!
Maryann	Well. I suppose. In a way.
Adam	Good, not evil, Maryann. Hear that? That's the new me!
Maryann	Uh huh.
Adam	Oh! And Judy! Ye'll never guess where I ended up?
Judy	Where?
Adam	I went tooootally over the rainbow. And Dad was the Great and Powerful Oz! And Judy I met oor Mam. And she telt me that if I was a good boy I'd be able tae get back tae see her.
Judy	That's great, Adam.
Adam	So I've decided, Jude. I ken howtay fix everythin.
Judy	How's that?
Adam	Me, you and Maryann. Livin together. And it'll be alright. Everythin will be alright again.
Judy	Adam, that's-
Maryann	Judith. I. Won't…
Judy	It wouldn't work, Adam.

Adam   Course it would. It'd be like Friends. You could Monica.
            Maryann could be Pheebs. I could be Chandler. Could I
            be anymore like Chandler?

Judy   That time has passed, Adam.

Adam   Don't say that. Time can slowed down. Time can be all
            different things. I should know, Judy. Used to be able tae
            control it.

Judy   Adam, you don't understand. I had to get away from….

            I've been lookin after you my whole life. I haven't ever
            been able to do things that other women my age do. I
            never had the time. And the time that I did have I was
            tryin to fight against things that I thought were wrong in
            the world. But that only took me so far, Adam. None of it
            made me. Happy.

Adam   And now?

Judy   And now…

She takes Maryann's hand.

            You need to let me have this. And it needs to be mine.

Adam   But. It could be. Like. Friends…?

Judy   Maryann couldn't live with you, Adam. Not after what
            you did to her in Glasgow.

Adam   That right, Maryann?

Maryann stands and goes to the window.

Adam   But that wasn't me. That was the bad me. This is the good me!

Judy   She's afraid of you. *I'm* afraid of you.

Adam presses his face into the pillow.

Adam   No.

Enter a stream of well-wishers, with all their noise and excitement.

Reporter   Falkirk Herald, Adam. How does it feel to be recovering?

Adam   Jobbies.

Reporter   What was going through your mind during the attack?

Adam   Bohemian Rhapsody.

Reporter   And are you aware you've been nominated for a Heroic Citizen award?

Adam   (*mimicking the song*) No no no no no no no no no no!

Bonnie's Mum   I just wantay say thank you for defendin ma lassie, ma Bonnie, against those animals. She's workin the day so she cannay get in, but don't think we don't know whit ye did for her.

Adam   Oh mama mia, mama mia!

Angie   Just so ye know, ye can take as long as ye want comin back to work.

We're gonnay make ye Employee of the Month as well, Adam. Would ye like that?

Adam   Nothing really matters. Anyone can see. Nothing really matters.

Nothing really matters.

To me…

MC   Upper Second Class Honours in Radiology: Steven Graham.

Adam claps tiredly.

Adam   When's Jude on, Maryann?

Maryann faces away from him, flicks through the programme.

Maryann   Quite soon, I think.

Adam   This is really borin.

Maryann   It is, isn't it?

Adam   I mean, is that all ye get a degree for? Walkin on stage, takin a scroll, and not fallin down?

Maryann   Well, there's a little bit more to it than that.

MC   Lower Second Class Honours in Cognitive Therapy: Louise Andrews.

Adam   So. Maryann.

Maryann   Uh-huh?

Adam   Are we friends?

Maryann looks up at him, hesitates. But then she's distracted.

Maryann   Oh, there she is!

MC   First Class Honours in Social Science: Judith Spark.

Adam and Maryann applaud and whoop.

Adam   Did you see her, Maryann?

Maryann   I did, Adam.

Adam   That was Jude. That was Our Jude!

Maryann   Ours. (*nods*) Ours.

Jude comes running over, gleeful, hugs Maryann and Adam in turn.

Judy   Did you see me? Did you see me up there? A first! I've got a first class degree!

Adam   Wow. That means your degree will arrive *much* quicker! Proud of you, Judy.

Maryann   We both are.

Adam   Aye. Both of us.

They all share an awkward moment, but one not without its warmth.

Oh, here, Judy. Got ye a grad-yoo-ay-shin present.

Judy   Is it a Queen CD?

Adam   Ye're no that lucky.

He hands her a box. She opens it.

Judy   Are these the same...?

It's the red shoes.

Adam   Aye.

Judy   I wonder if they still fit me.

She takes off her shoes, tries the new ones on.

Maryann   Perfect.

Adam   Ye're no gonnay give them back again, are ye?

Judy   Not this time. Thanks, Adam, they're a lovely gift.

Adam   Well, they're not from me, remember. They're from Mam.

Judy hugs him.

Adam   Have ye got a job sorted then?

Maryann   She's going to be a social worker.

Adam   Whit's that?

Judy   It's someone who helps families that need a bit of... support.

Bonnie enters. Clearly pregnant. Jude sees her.

Jude   Speaking of which...

                Right, Maryann. Shall we, um, make way?

Maryann   Yeah, let's get you home. Maybe see just how First Class you really are... (*smirks*)

Jude   See you soon, Adam.

Adam   Will ye be comin tae visit me soon, Jude?

Jude   (*nods towards Bonnie*) Oh, I think I'll be comin to visit more than just you.

                Okay, how we getting back?

Maryann   Taxi?

Jude   Actually, I've got a better idea.

She takes Maryann's hand, closes her eyes, clicks her heels together three times.

                There's no place like home.

They disappear.

Bonnie sees Adam, approaches.

Adam   Bonnie!

Bonnie   So sorry I'm late, Adam. Did I miss yer sister's graduation?

Adam   Aye, but that's alright. It was really borin anyway. Loadsay clappin just so Judy could get a First Class stamp. Dunno why she didn't go to the Post Office like everyone else.

Bonnie   Just y'know, havin difficulty walkin, gettin on and off buses that kinday thing.

Adam   How come?

Bonnie   Has nobody told ye?

Adam   Told me whit?

Bonnie   Guess.

Adam   Is it cos of whit them Animalz did to ye?

Bonnie   Naw, it's no that. They didn't hurt me. But thanks for defendin me, Adam. I was so scared.

Adam   Me tae.

Bonnie   Ye didnay look it.

Adam   Really?

Bonnie   Naw. You were very... heroic.

Adam takes her hand.

Adam   I like bein a hero. For you.

Bonnie   (*pause*) *Just* for me?

Adam   Whit do ye mean?

Bonnie   There's somethin I have to tell ye. I didn't wantay before,
            cos ye'd just got out of hospital and you were recoverin
            and all that. But em.

Adam   Whit?

Bonnie   Well. It's, uh, pressin against ye right now.

Adam   Ye've put on a bittay weight? That's alright, Bonnie, I
            don't mind. Seen the size of ma sister?

Bonnie   It's no weight, Adam, it's…

She whispers in his ear. He looks at her stomach.

Adam   I'm gonnay be…?

Bonnie   Uh-huh.

Adam   And you're gonnay be…?

Bonnie   Aye.

Adam   So we're gonnay be…?

Bonnie   That's right.

Adam   C'mon, Bonnie, we've got work to do.

Bonnie   Where we going?

Adam   To do my duty. Somewhere soon, Bonnie, a child will be
            in trouble… crying…and I'll have to wipe his arse.

(*addresses the audience*)

But Falkirk? If you ever need me? Just use the Sparky Signal.

A rainbow appears across the stage.

Big, swelling, orchestral superhero music. Adam rips open his shirt to reveal a rippling costume, an 'A' on his chest.

Adam   Bye, dudes.

Bonnie   Byeee! Sorry, everyone. (*pats her belly*) We kinda need him now.

Adam   Okay, Bonnie, hold on tight. Ready?

Bonnie   Ready.

Adam   Cos we're going way up high.

They take off into the air. Whoosh!

Light fades, save for the rainbow.

Brief musical refrain from 'Somewhere Over the Rainbow'

END